David Hill

The social influence of Christianity : with special reference to contemporary problems

David Hill

The social influence of Christianity : with special reference to contemporary problems

ISBN/EAN: 9783337261474

Printed in Europe, USA, Canada, Australia, Japan

Cover: Foto ©Lupo / pixelio.de

More available books at **www.hansebooks.com**

The Social Influence
of Christianity

With Special Reference to Contemporary Problems.

BY

DAVID J. HILL, LL.D.,
President of the University of Rochester.

THE NEWTON LECTURES FOR 1887.

Let him that stole steal no more: but rather let him labor, working with his hands the thing which is good, that he may have to give to him that needeth. — SAINT PAUL.

BOSTON :
SILVER, BURDETT & COMPANY,
110–112 BOYLSTON STREET.
1894.

TO

My Mother,

CATHARINE J. PACKER,

THIS VOLUME IS LOVINGLY DEDICATED.

PREFACE.

THIS volume consists of eight lectures delivered before the Newton Theological Institution, in May, 1887, at the invitation of the president and faculty, and through the liberality of the Hon. J. W. Merrill. The lectures are now published at the request of the president, faculty, and students, and constitute the second published volume of "Newton Lectures," the first being "The Hebrew Feasts," by Professor William Henry Green, D.D., LL.D., of Princeton Theological Seminary.

The lecturer was permitted to supplement his general preparation as a teacher of political economy and sociology during the past ten years, by six months of travel and observation in the principal countries of central and southern Europe with these lectures constantly in view, and by six months of special reading in the literature collected before and during his journey.

He desires to make public acknowledgment of the sustained interest shown by all who attended the course of lectures, and especially of the personal courtesy and hospitality of President Hovey and the members of the faculty during his pleasant visit at Newton.

CONTENTS.

		PAGE
I.	WHAT IS HUMAN SOCIETY?	9
II.	WHAT HAS CHRISTIANITY DONE FOR SOCIETY?	35
III.	CHRISTIANITY AND THE PROBLEMS OF LABOR	65
IV.	CHRISTIANITY AND THE PROBLEMS OF WEALTH	95
V.	CHRISTIANITY AND THE PROBLEMS OF MARRIAGE	127
VI.	CHRISTIANITY AND THE PROBLEMS OF EDUCATION	157
VII.	CHRISTIANITY AND THE PROBLEMS OF LEGISLATION	187
VIII.	CHRISTIANITY AND THE PROBLEMS OF REPRESSION	211

[For detailed analysis see page preceding the beginning of each lecture.]

I.

WHAT IS HUMAN SOCIETY?

WHAT IS HUMAN SOCIETY?

1. Preliminary Questions.
2. The twofold View of the Sophists.

I. THE NATURALISTIC CONCEPTION OF SOCIETY.
1. Plato's Theory.
2. Aristotle's Theory.
3. Naturalistic Doctrines in Modern Times.
    (1) Montesquieu; (2) Condorcet; (3) Kant; (4) Quetelet; (5) Buckle.
4. Biological Sociology.
    (1) Spencer; (2) Schaefile; (3) Espinas; (4) Mulford.
5. Inadequacy of the Naturalistic Conception.

II. THE IDEALISTIC CONCEPTION OF SOCIETY.
1. Rousseau's Social Contract.
2. The Theocratic Conception.
3. The Kingdom of God.
4. Christian Society.
5. The Ideal in the Formation of Society.

III. THE SYNTHESIS OF THE NATURAL AND THE IDEAL IN SOCIETY.
1. Society founded in Human Wants.
2. Society modified by Human Wills.
3. Society perfected through Ideals.
4. Answer to the question, What is human society?

THE SOCIAL INFLUENCE OF CHRISTIANITY.

I.

WHAT IS HUMAN SOCIETY?

1. An accurate conception of the nature of society is an essential prerequisite to any valuable discussion of its problems. This conception may be obtained by resolving society into its elementary constituents and discovering the forces and laws by which these elements are united. Human society is composed of individual human beings, who may be considered as its atomic units. The process of analysis is very simple, but the forces of social synthesis and the laws of their action present materials of great complexity. Does the cause of association lie in the human individual, or does it pertain to the environment in which individuals are placed? Does it originate from conscious volition, or does it proceed from organic constitution? Does it admit of voluntary counteraction and resistance, or does it produce its results by necessity? These are questions which must be answered before we can solve any social problem whatever; for, if the will of man is not in

any sense the cause of society, it is difficult to imagine how it can transform, or even slightly modify, the social structure.

These preliminary questions reduce themselves to one, which may be formulated thus: What is the relation of individuals to the social whole; is it that of living parts united by natural laws into a greater organism, or is it that of voluntary members freely choosing their form of association? More briefly still, Is society a natural organism, or is it a voluntary group formed by contract?

2. We may trace from a great antiquity two distinct and opposing conceptions created in answer to this question. The Greek Sophists, who raised nearly all the questions which men have since been trying to answer, divided the world into two parts: one ruled by the inflexible laws of nature, the other governed by the freewill of man.[1] They considered a part of our human laws as arbitrary or conventional; others, as derived from the constitution of man, and hence the projection of inanimate nature, independent of volition and wholly unalterable. Upon this fundamental distinction have been erected two different theories of society, which we may designate as the Naturalistic Theory and the Idealistic Theory.

I.

1. Although Plato is best known as an idealist, his social theory belongs to the naturalistic type. For

[1] For this doctrine of the Sophists, see Plato's Laws, 889. The best translation is Jowett's.

him society is a product of nature, a creature of instinct and environment. Organic need is the determining cause of social, as it is of animal, organization.[2] The division of labor in the sphere of industrial production was fully understood by Plato, and its origin was referred to the diversity of natural powers and aptitudes. A state, he taught, is a living body, similar to an individual organism. Its different classes are like the various faculties of an individual being, and it is endowed with a soul — an emanation of the universal reason. Its growth and decay, its diseases and its conflicts of function, are similar to those of a living man. But as nature is the creation of God, so also is society. As there is an ideal for the individual man, whose highest attainment is perfect virtue, so there is an ideal for the State, the perfect republic. This ideal Plato attempted to picture. It is a community in which the wise govern, in which virtue, as he conceived it, is universally cultivated by the union of the best and the elimination of the base, and yet involving the destruction of the family and its affections, the perpetuation of the militant spirit, and the laudation of a narrow nationalism. This most visionary of idealists is still the most radical of realists. The members of the social body are wholly devoid of spontaneity. The realization of the ideal must come from God alone, whose agent is the wise man clothed with power. Little did Plato dream that this "wise man"

---

[2] For Plato's ideas on the nature of society, see his Republic, translated by Jowett.

was hoped for and expected by the Hebrew people, the Deliverer and Messiah, who should bring to earth, not the narrow national supremacy desired by both Plato and the Hebrews, but the perfect kingdom for which the world was waiting.

2. Aristotle approaches the question of the nature of society with all of Plato's realism, but without his ideal tendencies. For Aristotle the State is the product of nature, and he proceeds to study it from a natural point of view.[3] He points out an important fact, that the individual cannot exist in isolation. He finds the social unit not in the individual, but in the pair, the family. But this unit is not an atom; it is composite; it is already an organism, a living molecule whose parts could not subsist alone. This is a fertile conception. It draws society within the boundaries of biology. Society is no longer a dead thing, but a living being. Since it is a living organism, it is subjected to the laws of birth and death, of growth and dissolution, which rule all life. Change is its essential condition. Every attempt, then, to impose upon it an immutable constitution must prove chimerical. Societies differ according to their times and according to their environments. No constitution can be adapted to all peoples. Again, no living being is composed of wholly similar parts. Society ought to be composed of parts which are separated from one another by differences. This is why the family, Aristotle's social element, is

[3] For Aristotle's philosophy of society, see his Politics, translated by Jowett.

formed of heterogeneous constituents: man, woman, and children. That difference is the condition of their union. Here is not only diversity, but subordination, gradation of power, a scale of authority; the woman obeying the man, and the child the woman. In this rudimentary society is the beginning of government. The father becomes the patriarch, the patriarch the king. Thus is developed the social organism. Nature ordains these differences, from them grows the equilibrium of the whole people; and so society exists, not by convention and choice, but by inherent constitution and necessity. Each individual finds himself at birth a part of a social whole which neither he nor any other man has created. Without this preëxisting environment he would not be what he is. He is, then, himself the creature of society rather than its creator. Its language, its traditions, its customs, its laws, combine to shape him and to determine his individuality. How fully this idea was accepted by the Greeks is evident from the value they put upon culture as essential to the making of a man, and also from their word ἰδιώτης, which first meant a "private man," then a "clumsy fellow," and at last a "fool," an "idiot."

We may summarize the whole doctrine of pagan antiquity as being in its final conclusions a naturalistic and organic theory of society. Without arriving at the definite biological conception that prevails in modern sociology, Greek thought distinctly grasped the idea that society is created by forces outside of man himself, yet operating through him as their necessary organ, thus producing not merely an aggregate but a living organism.

3. To follow in detail the history of social theories would certainly prove wearisome, and probably would efface the memory of the most important outlines by filling the mind with insignificant refinements. And yet we cannot do justice to the naturalistic school without a passing notice of the progress it has made.

(1) In Montesquieu's epoch-making "Spirit of the Laws" we find the naturalistic conception prevailing.[4] He regards the organization of society as reposing less on human ideas than on instinctive impulsions — such as the sense of dependence on others, the need of aliments, the sexual attachment, and the sympathetic inclinations. Though the State is for the great French jurist the work of mind, its roots reach down into physical conditions out of which it is developed. The laws express this origin and are but the reflex of the natural environment.

(2) Condorcet emphasized this tendency of thought by proposing that the methods of the physical sciences be applied also to moral and social phenomena.[5] He taught that human progress is subject to physical laws and capable of even mathematical treatment. To measure social phenomena in order to discover their laws; to draw from the knowledge of their laws the foreknowledge of future phenomena; to found

---

[4] Montesquieu, Esprit des Lois, livre i, chapitre ii.

[5] Condorcet, Esquisse d'un Tableau historique des progrès de l'Esprit Humain.

upon that foreknowledge combinations and preventions which would secure the amelioration of the human race, — such was Condorcet's doctrine of the task and the power of social science.

(3) Although Immanuel Kant made absolute freedom the masterpiece of his metaphysics, he regarded the world of phenomena as ruled by invariable laws. In the marvelous harmonies of nature he discerned a secret conspiracy of forces which is, indeed, mechanical, but at the same time the expression of a superior will. Human actions were for him determined in great part by general laws of nature. He thought that, as "the laws of the variation of the atmosphere are constant, though no particular can be foreseen at a given point, and in the mass they occasion in a uniform manner and without interruption the growth of plants, the course of streams, and all the other occurrences of the natural economy," so the social phenomena — births and deaths, marriages and divorces — are subject to natural laws.[6] We may trace similar ideas in the writings of Fichte and Hegel, who gave them abundant illustration mingled with the vagaries of a fanciful subjectivism, and especially in those of Herder, who first applied the principle of natural evolution to history and claimed for it the character of an exact science.

(4) Very important additions were made to social science by the Belgian mathematician, Quetelet, who by measurements and statistics sought to demonstrate the uniformity of social phenomena. His

---

[6] Kant, Allgemeine Naturgeschichte.

methods are too technical for popular exposition, but he may be accorded the distinction of having raised statistics to the dignity of a science. His "Social Physics" is a memorable contribution to the science of man and of society. His tables show that acts of the most personal and apparently spontaneous nature are measurable by general rules. For example, the number of murders committed in France in six successive years, from 1826 to 1831 inclusive, shows a very slight variation; and the proportion of the instruments of destruction employed is about the same from year to year. Thus, for five successive years the number of murders committed with a gun or pistol does not vary more than eight, the absolute numbers being 56, 64, 60, 61, and 57. Such observations led Quetelet to maintain that "society encloses in itself the germ of the crimes that are committed. It is society itself, in a certain sense, that prepares them, and the criminal is only the instrument who executes them. The social state, then, supposes a certain order of crimes, which result as a necessary consequence from its organization."[7] I do not pause to criticize either the logic or the ethics of this reasoning, but note it as a stage in the development of sociology.

(5) Buckle has attempted the construction of a history of civilization on the assumption "that the moral actions of men are the product, not of their volition, but of their antecedents." Social progress,

---

[7] Quetelet, Physique Sociale; ou, Essai sur le Développement des Facultés de l'Homme.

he says, is "the result of large and general causes which, working upon the aggregate of society, produce certain consequences without regard to the volition of those particular men of whom the society is composed."[8] These "large and general causes" are "climate, food, soil, and the general aspect of nature." Here volition is absolutely excluded as a factor of progress. Quetelet explains social phenomena as produced through human volition, but Buckle takes the higher ground that human volition is wholly excluded from effecting social changes. He was clearly a more loyal determinist than he was a faithful observer.

4. It has been reserved for our age to erect a complete sociology upon a purely naturalistic basis, treating society as a natural growth, a veritable organism in the strictest sense of the word, as little dependent upon human volition as any example in the animal series.

(1) For Herbert Spencer, sociology is simply an extension of biology.[9] He has come upon societies long before arriving at man in the order of evolution. Every individual animal, he affirms, is a society, composed of living constituents. The individuality of an animal, far from excluding that of its component elements, supposes and requires it. Organic composition is simply a union of living parts into more extended living wholes. Man is an individual only in

[8] Buckle's History of Civilization in England.
[9] Spencer's Illustrations of Universal Progress, essay on The Social Organism; and Principles of Sociology.

a relative sense. He is really a society of smaller individuals. His unity is the result of their organization. He is thus either identical with them or a result of their combination. When dissolution takes place he is no more. These constituents have been differentiated and specialized so that each class has its own function. Human society is to individual men what a single man is to the living cells of his body. It is more than an aggregate, it is a veritable organism. It is not formed by voluntary association any more than an animal body is, but by the unconscious grouping of individual men acting according to the laws of their nature. Human society is, therefore, simply an "episode of universal evolution," as necessary as a crystal and as little the work of will.

(2) Spencer's principal difficulty in completing the analogy between society and an animal organism is thus expressed by himself: "The parts of an animal form a concrete whole; but the parts of a society form a whole that is discrete. While the living units composing the whole are bound together in close contact in the animal, the living units composing society are free, not in contact, and more or less widely dispersed." Spencer's attempts to explain away this disparity are not so successful as those of the German sociologist, Schaeffle, in his "Structure and Life of the Social Body." In that exhaustive work, the learned author shows that in every animal organism there is an intercellular substance, which is not composed of the living cells, but acts as a means of separation and communication between them.

The discontinuity of the parts of the social body is not, therefore, a fatal objection to its being considered as an organism, since this is quite in analogy with the structure of animal bodies. The roads, railways, and telegraphic lines of human society serve to bring its constituents into practical coherence, as the nerves of sensation do in the animal body. That these were a late development is quite in analogy with biological history, in which the formation of a nervous system marks an advanced stage of animal evolution.

(3) The finishing touch to the naturalistic theory seems to have been given by the French zoölogist, Espinas, who, in his " Animal Societies," discovers the necessity and the fact of association in the lowest orders of the animal creation, and supplies many data in tracing the evolution of human society from the rudimentary social life of the inferior animals. " No living being," says Espinas, " is alone. The animals in particular sustain numerous relations with the existences which surround them ; and, without speaking of those which live in permanent commerce with their kind, almost all are constrained by biological necessities to contract, though it be for a brief period, an intimate union with some other individual of their species." [10]

(4) Thus the lowest forms of life and human society are connected as products of natural forces operating under a law of evolution. Society is, then, the greatest of animals. But we are led a step

[10] Espinas, Des Sociétés Animales.

beyond this. In his book on "The Nation," the late Dr. Mulford says: "The physical organism is determined in itself by a law of necessity, as the tree which cannot be other than it is; the ethical organism is determined in a law of freedom, which is the condition of moral action. . . . The conditions of history presume the being of the nation as a moral organism. History is not a succession of separate events and actions, but a development in a moral order, and in the unity and continuity of a life which moves on unceasingly, as some river in its unbroken current. It is only as the nation is an organism that this unity and continuity is manifest in it, and as a moral organism that this moral order is confirmed in it."[11] Dr. Mulford then adds: "The nation is a moral personality." So it seems that a society is not simply a great animal, but a great *person*. All this may be very true, but I cannot resist the feeling that in some way we have passed out of the sphere of science into a cloudland of mythology, when the nation is endowed with personality. If we have shrunk from Auguste Comte's apotheosis of Humanity as the Supreme Being, how shall we treat this "moral person" to whom Dr. Mulford's speculative mind has introduced us? How august and majestic this "moral person" must be, to whom we all stand in the relation of microscopic cells to a human body! Has biology, then, a new religion? But the moment I try to regain my own sense of personality, which seems swallowed up in this "moral

---

[11] E. Mulford's The Nation, chap. i.

person," I find myself in trouble. I do not see how a person can be composed of *other* persons. He would be a *congress*, not a person. If a person cannot be composed of other persons, then this "moral person," which society is said to be, is either not a person at all, or else is a person apart from its constituents, individual men. In the latter case we have a new divinity who is a separate personal being, the soul of the nation. This brings us back to Plato. But if a person cannot be composed solely of other organisms, then I, as a person, am something apart from the constituent cells that form my body. I am a society *plus* personality. Now, admitting that society is an organism, that is, made up of other organisms, there is something in society that is not organism, the individual personalities that inhabit the constituent organisms themselves. Here we come upon a great truth. It is that the organic theory of society leaves out of account this element of personality that belongs to every human individual. As for Dr. Mulford's "moral person," that is but the creature of the power of abstraction. It is the personification, merely, of the social bond — the mythologizing tendency that peopled the Pantheon with creatures of the fancy, alive in the nineteenth century and creating a national divinity. This "moral person" can nowhere be found, except in the individual men of the nation. But each of these men consciously knows in himself a personality that is neither the sum nor the product of his component parts. He is an organism *plus* a person. More precisely, *he is a person in an organism*.

(5) Admitting the truth of the naturalistic theory of society, as far as it goes, except the completeness of it, we seem to have missed some important factor. That factor is personality. However we may doubt the personality of Dr. Mulford's " moral person," we cannot doubt that we ourselves are persons. The question, then, is: What have persons contributed to the constitution of society, beyond what natural forces have contributed? The naturalistic sociology is merely one of observation and induction. It can observe and report social facts. It cannot do more. It cannot explain progress, which is the one preëminently important social phenomenon. It cannot determine, by its purely physical methods, what *ought to be*, or that *anything* " ought to be." It is utterly powerless to solve any social problem, because its fundamental postulate is that the will and intellect of man have no initiative power, either to create or transform society. As for social responsibility, there can be none for the naturalistic theory. All is determined by natural necessity, and, upon this assumption, " Whatever is, is right."

II.

1. The missing factor in the naturalistic conception of society is human personality. Man is a force other than physical nature, conscious of himself and of his power, reacting upon and transforming his environment, partly its master and not wholly its creature. This is the assumption of Rousseau, who,

though not without predecessors in proclaiming this truth, is its most celebrated modern advocate among social theorists. Modern republicanism is a political movement, based on the dignity and essential freedom of human nature, on the fact and the potency of personality. It is incompatible with pure and absolute naturalism, which teaches the doctrine that "might makes right" under the milder formula of the "struggle for existence and the survival of the fittest." Rousseau is the philosopher of republicanism. He assumes certain inherent and inalienable rights in man ; that is, his possession of personality, without which he could not have rights, and his ethical nature, without which he could not know them. Rousseau conceives society as having been instituted by a "social contract," a compact voluntarily formed by free agents, in order to secure the protection of their rights by union and reciprocity. Their primary equality, their personal freedom, and their pursuit of an ideal are all involved in this theory.[12] But Rousseau embarrassed the truth with cumbrous impedimenta of error. The "state of nature" is for him an atomistic condition of existence, in which men are imagined as wandering in isolation, without interrelations, without institutions, and without laws. It has been easy for the naturalistic school to show that such a condition of human life is impossible, and such historical critics as Sir Henry Maine and such political theorists as Bluntschli have rejected it as not only unhistoric but utterly fanciful. To refute

---

[12] Rousseau, Contrat Social, livre i, chapitre iv.

Rousseau's doctrine of the origin of society, however, is by no means to show that voluntary contract has not been a transforming element in social progress. Society is not the creation of a day, but the growth of centuries. History shows that men have acted in the formation of new societies and in the reconstruction of old ones under the guidance of an ideal whose abstract formula is voluntary contract. I believe that Rousseau is correct in maintaining that men have made society what it is by following a pattern that was an idea before it was a reality.

2. If we care to retrace the idealistic conception of society to its source, we shall find its origin among the ancient Hebrews. The theocracy instituted by Moses, a kingdom without a human king, a commonwealth built on worship, was held together by the allegiance of the people; and, while its constitution was divinely ordained, membership in it was a voluntary adherence. Moses erected a moral ideal, established a ceremonial to give it vitality, and appealed to men to realize it by submitting to theocratic laws. Apostasy was always possible, and sometimes chosen. The Hebrew commonwealth, in its beginning, was essentially a form of association based on voluntary recognition of a moral ideal. It never lost this character. The Judges served to give personality and form to the moral and religious union of the people, but they could not unify and concentrate the Hebrew nation. After the loss of nationality, the political feebleness of the commonwealth in the midst of powerful monarchies was keenly felt. Samuel be-

came virtual king of Israel, a king who ruled the conscience and swayed the whole moral nature of his people. "He seems to have entertained the magnificent but impracticable conception," says Dr. J. H. Allen, "that the real and acknowledged sovereign of Israel should be the invisible Divinity and Protector, whose arm had guarded the nation in so many perils, whose Spirit had from the first commissioned and inspired its faithful men; and that the actual ruler should be only, as it were, a regent, or viceroy, of this unseen sovereign."[13] Accordingly, he erected into the permanence and power of an institution the prophetic function, by the establishment of the "Schools of the Prophets." Out of this institution of prophecy came those predictions and expectations of the Prince of Peace, the spiritual sovereign, who should be at once king and deliverer, the realized hope of Israel. No doubt it was with heavy heart, made heavier by the disappointments that followed, that Samuel saw the necessity of choosing a human king. The king was appointed and Samuel's fears were realized. Thus the theocracy that had been a fact with Moses and a reminiscence with Samuel, became for the prophets a splendid dream of the future. The throne never ceased to feel the power of the school. Exposure and denunciation of wrong, exposition and proclamation of justice, even interference with the royal counsels and the authoritative dictation of policy, became the functions of the prophets, who continually voiced forth and empha-

---

[13] J. H. Allen's Hebrew Men and Times, chap. iii.

sized the ideals of the theocracy. "Both in their own and in the popular belief, they were in the strictest sense ambassadors and representatives, to speak before the nation messages from the invisible and dread majesty of its King."

3. Out of that "goodly fellowship of the prophets" came the Messianic predictions which rendered possible the mission of Christ's forerunner. "The kingdom of heaven is at hand!" cried John in the wilderness. He came not from books and circles of scholars, as if his message were a discovery of learning; not from courts and councils, as if it were an induction gathered from political policies, but from the solitudes of the desert, as if to announce a proclamation from God himself. Christ appeared, to fulfill his words and interpret their meaning. "My kingdom is not of this world," he said, yet "the kingdom of God is within you." It is a kingdom for this world, though not of it. He taught his disciples to pray: "Thy kingdom come, thy will be done in earth as it is in heaven." That prayer and its answer have gradually transformed and are transforming human society. The old order which Plato and Aristotle saw about them was not a wholly necessary or permanent order. Through the teachings of Christ the theocratic idea of society which Moses taught the ancient Hebrews, which Samuel loved but could not perpetuate in its purity, which the prophets steadily held before the world for centuries, and which the Christian ministry has diffused throughout the globe, has become the confessed

faith of all civilized nations, who accept it because they are civilized, and are civilized because they accept it. For these millions, higher and more potent than any human king is the "King Invisible." His will is the ideal of society, and must be discovered and obeyed. Henceforth men conceive that society is to be shaped by the conformity of individual wills to a divine will. It is the organized assent of persons to the plan of a Person. It is no longer the product of nature alone, the creature of cosmic forces acting in accordance with necessary laws. Its climax is not in the realization of a "moral person" whose substance is the nation, but in conformity to an infinite righteousness whose substance is the living God.

4. Christ not only introduced what was to the pagan world a new idea of society, but he proposed to create a new society. What was his method? "It was," says Dr. Fairbairn, "to work from within outward, from the one to the many, from the unit to the mass. He proceeded by calling individuals, for their own sakes indeed, yet not for their own sakes only, but for man's as well. Christ, in order that the truth and life in him might live and work, created out of the men he called and saved a society, the kingdom of heaven, the city of God. . . . The society of the saved was intended to be a society of the healed, working like a great healthful balm in the sick heart of humanity."[14] Was it not his aim

---

[14] A. M. Fairbairn's The City of God, part iii; Discourse on Christ in History.

that this society should ultimately absorb and transfigure human society? Has Christianity, then, no relation to social problems? Is not its relation that of leaven to the loaf, a perfect solution of social problems by a thorough permeation and transformation? If not, why should we continue to pray against hope, "Thy kingdom come"?

5. We have found among the Hebrews a conception of society based upon a realizable ideal. While it is in part in perfect contrast to the prevailing pagan conception, it does not altogether exclude the notion of society as a natural product and essentially an organism. It would seem, on the contrary, that the Hebrew doctrine of God's relation to the world as Creator and Providence would involve likewise his authorship of society. In truth, the Hebrew commonwealth was regarded as his particular creation, and it was held to differ from other societies in being throughout of divine constitution. But the voluntary element was always uppermost in the Hebrew mind. God "chose" his people, and his people also "chose" him. "Choose you this day, whom ye will serve," implies the presence of volition in the union with the commonwealth. The human will was even more distinctly recognized by Christ. "Ye will not come to me, that ye might have life," marks the entrance into the kingdom of heaven, not, indeed, as resulting from volition, but as impossible without it. If we accept the psychology of Christ, we shall hold that certain forms of association are based upon consent, or covenant, and that society is composed of

persons who do not act solely from necessity. Society may also be an organism. Paul does not hesitate to describe a spiritual society in the terms of organic analogy. "For as we have many members in one body, and all members have not the same office; so we, being many, are one body in Christ; and every one members one of another." And the Church is called "the body" of Christ. But we must not forget that this body is composed of those who have willingly become its parts, and that unconscious or involuntary constituents are wholly beyond the scope of its inclusion. Those who "would not come" that they "might have life" were excluded from that body, the Church, in which the life of Christ is supposed especially to reside. The very notion of the kingdom of God implies a conscious and voluntary entrance into it. "Repent ye, repent ye," is the herald's cry, as he invites men to enter the coming kingdom, as if the very foundation of that new society depended upon the mental acts of its possible constituents. And thus has been vindicated in the field of history by the growth of that ever-coming kingdom, and even more fully by its variant forms of polity illustrated in the development of the Church, the power of men to pursue, and in part to realize, a social ideal, to associate themselves by contract and covenant for purposes dear to themselves, and to constitute a society of which nature is not the cause, and which is a living organism only as it embodies a life that is not a product of itself.

III.

We are now prepared to make a rapid synthesis of the elements that constitute society and to answer our main question: What is its nature?

1. Man is a being of numerous instinctive wants, whose satisfaction requires his association with others of his kind. Endowed with reason and articulate speech, men naturally seek companionship. Sympathy also serves to draw men together, and affection weaves its invisible but powerful network about them. Three preëminent needs are constant and universal with men, holding together even the incommunicative, the unsympathetic, and those without true affection. They are: (1) The need of physical comforts, which gives rise to *economic* institutions; (2) the need of sexual companionship, which gives rise to the *domestic* institution; and (3) the need of protection from enemies and the rapacious, which gives rise to *political* institutions. These are the "social bonds" which, more than any others, hold individuals together in society. Thus the rudiments of society are formed by nature.

2. Men are also endowed with will, and in satisfying these needs, they may regard or ignore the laws of normal conduct. They may satisfy their physical appetites by labor, theft, or slavery. They may establish their sexual relations upon the basis of monogamy or upon that of polygamy. They may protect themselves by private wars, by servile submission to a chief who will promise them safety, or

by the enactment of just laws to be executed by public officers. It is because the will of man may modify the rudimentary society established by nature, that there are social problems.

3. But man is not simply a compound of instinctive wants and self-determining will. He is also endowed with intellect, by which he can create and comprehend ideals both of private and public action. The real progress of society is attained in the gradual realization of these ideals by their incorporation into life. The problems of society in every age are, how to render the ideal actual in the performance of social functions.

4. Our answer to the question, What is human society? is this: It is a composite product of (1) natural wants, (2) human wills, and (3) moral ideals. The human society of to-day is the result of association prompted by human wants, which are formulated by human wills, through the partial appropriation of moral ideals. The reconstruction or transformation of society must proceed upon a clear comprehension of the natural basis of society in the instinctive wants of man, the mode in which the human will can affect the performance of social functions, and the motives for the conformity of the popular will to the ideals of a higher social life.

I can never think of the relation of Christianity to social problems without seeing before my mind's eye that powerful picture of Hofmann's that hangs in the gallery at Dresden, representing the youthful Christ in the Temple, surrounded by the Jewish doctors. In the midst of that throng of shrewd yet puzzled faces, wearing the venerable aspect of authority, the gentle youth stands a little apart, his sad, intellectual features softened with a smile of unutterable sweetness, his high, pure brow and white, glistening garments radiating a light that seems to palpitate with life and to chase away every shadow within the sweep of its illumination. He stands there like a heavenly messenger who has just arrived from the effulgence of the throne of God upon some earthly embassy. The doctors of the law are silent before him. They wait, as if in awe, for the parting of his boyish lips. It is the picture of the living Christ opening to mortal eyes the vision of God's coming kingdom. Thus to earth's sovereigns and jurisconsults and doctrinaires and social theorists Christ unfolds the divine ideals of human society, while the waiting world is hushed into silence by the spell of his power and hangs its hopes upon his words of life.

11.
WHAT HAS CHRISTIANITY DONE FOR SOCIETY?

WHAT HAS CHRISTIANITY DONE FOR SOCIETY?

I. WHAT IS CHRISTIANITY?
   1. As an Ethical Doctrine and Life.
   2. As an Influence touching the whole Nature.
   3. The Method of Christianity.

II. THE SOCIAL FUNCTIONS AFFECTED BY CHRISTIANITY.
   1. Possibility of tracing the Social Influence of Christianity.
   2. The Functions of Society:
      (1) The Industrial;
      (2) The Domestic;
      (3) The Political.

III. THE EFFECTS OF CHRISTIANITY UPON SOCIETY.
   1. Upon Labor and the Laborer:
      (1) By dignifying Labor;
      (2) By producing a Rehabilitation of Labor;
      (3) By destroying Slavery;
      (4) By consecrating Labor.
   2. Upon Wealth and its Uses:
      (1) Christ's Doctrine of Wealth.
      (2) Christian Beneficence.
      (3) Christianity and the Right of Property.
   3. Upon Marriage and Woman.
      (1) The Ancient Status of Woman.
      (2) The Germanic Status.
      (3) The Transformation of Marriage.
   4. Upon Children and Education.
      (1) The Ancient Status of Children.
      (2) The Character of Pagan Education.
      (3) The Establishment of Christian Schools.
   5. Upon Legislation.
      (1) In respect to Personal Status.
      (2) In respect to Personal Conduct.
   6. Upon Punishment.

II.

WHAT HAS CHRISTIANITY DONE FOR SOCIETY?

Having arrived at a conception of the nature of human society, we may ask, What has Christianity done for it? From this historical retrospect we may derive some aid in showing what more it can do in the future for society. As a preliminary, however, to both these inquiries, we must first ask, What do we mean by Christianity?

I.

1. Nothing is more difficult than to imprison within a brief verbal formula the essence of Christianity. It is hardly necessary for me to say that I nowhere intend to identify it with the Church. That would be to include a large element of human policy and even directly anti-Christian power. I can find no better expression of my idea of Christianity than to say that it is the influence of Jesus Christ. It is a double influence, that of a personal life and that of doctrinal teaching; of a life not less than of a doctrine, for the figure of Christ's person is not less conspicuous in the world's eye than the authority of his teaching. Indeed, it must be admitted that the authority of his doctrine proceeds from the nature of his person. Between them there is the most per-

fect union. The Evangelist, John, said: "In him was life, and the life was the light of men." That luminous life was a double one, in which the divine and the human were consciously united. His doctrine is the revelation of his life, translated into human language. It teaches the Fatherhood of God and the brotherhood of men, as realized in his own being. His conception of a perfect society is a state in which God is loved as Father, and men are loved as brethren. Hence, he sums up all human duty in that brief epitome of the law: "Thou shalt love the Lord thy God with all thy heart, and with all thy soul, and with all thy strength, and with all thy mind; and thy neighbour as thyself." We must not allow ourselves to fall into the barren scholasticism of regarding this summary as merely a new classification of duties. Its true originality is not in its abridgement of earlier ethical codes, but in the disclosure of the real essence of the human ideal. The emphasis of Christ's new promulgation of the law is not love *God*, or love *thy neighbor*, but *love* God, and *love* thy neighbor. *Love* is the essence of the law. It is not a classification of duties which Christ offers, but a new statement of the very substance of duty.

2. Christianity is the influence of that doctrine, and of the life in which it was perfectly exemplified, on the world. It has proved the most epoch-making influence that has ever been introduced into society. It has appealed to the intellect and to the heart with a power to which no other influence is comparable, at once enlightening the understanding and quickening

the sensibilities. There were other elements, however, in the influence of Christ as potent in commanding men as his ethical doctrine and his personal life. His miraculous power, his resurrection from the dead, his promise of immortality, his atonement for sin, must not be underestimated. They have given him a hold on men through the imagination, through the hopes of the heart, and through the consciousness of sin, that an ethical life and doctrine alone could never have secured. All these are included in any adequate conception of historical Christianity, and without them we can have no explanation of its power in the world.

3. I have already referred to Christ's method. His teachings were directed to individuals, but they are found in their ultimate implications to extend to society. The words of Christ have wonderful reverberating power. Without ever speaking of society as an object of interest to him, he has uttered truth that has affected it profoundly, because it has been reflected from personal to public life, until the precepts of private conduct have been reëchoed as the laws of nations. Christ taught the need of individual regeneration, and history shows that the regeneration of men is the regeneration of society. Taine simply restates a very ancient Christian truth when he says: "History is at bottom a problem of psychology."

II.

1. Can we disentangle from the fabric of history those threads which have been woven into it by the

influence of Jesus, and whose bright colors would not adorn it were it not for him? It is a difficult and a delicate task, and though I cannot hope to accomplish it completely, I believe that it will be possible to show that much that the world most highly values can be directly and unerringly traced back to this origin.

2. In order to exclude from notice those effects of Christianity that belong to the individual solely, and to confine ourselves to those which are strictly social, it will be necessary to enumerate the specific functions of society, and then to see how the influence of Jesus has affected them. Society is a state of association for the satisfaction of three universal needs: (1) The need of physical comforts; (2) the need of sexual companionship, and (3) the need of protection of rights. It performs, therefore, three functions: (1) The industrial, relating to means of sustaining or preserving men; (2) the domestic, relating to the means of multiplying or producing men, and (3) the political, relating to means of regulating or governing men.

(1) The industrial function presents two problems. The first is that of labor, or the production of subsistence. The second is that of wealth, or the distribution of subsistence. These two problems were especially difficult to solve at the time when Christ came into the world, when three fourths of the population of Rome were enrolled paupers and the inequalities which wealth had created held half the world in slavery.

(2) The domestic function also gives rise to two problems. The first is that of marriage, the condition of the increase of population, reduced to a merely nominal institution by the "free marriage" system and loose divorce laws of the Roman Empire. The second is education, or the development of the population, a truly domestic institution, since it begins in the family and is normally transferred only to one who stands in *loco parentis*. If the increase of life be detached from responsibility for the destiny of life, there can be no stable condition of society. For this reason education is normally a domestic institution.

(3) The political function also suggests two problems. The first is that of legislation, or the definition of rights. The second is that of repression, or the enforcement of rights.

III.

We shall see presently something of what Christianity has done for the solution of these vast problems with which all great minds have struggled. But, first of all, let us note with what new impulse Christianity began its work. Its apostles moved, as they thought, under the mandate of a divine imperative. Called by the voice of the Eternal, they went forth with the weight of the universe behind them. No men had ever before received such a vocation, and none had ever before such a sense of their mission. "Go teach all nations" implied that all nations could be taught; that there were in every man, under a skin of whatever color, whether bond or free, a reason and a conscience that bore in fractured outlines the lineaments of a God. No earthly conqueror had ever gone forth to conquer the hearts and wills of men. But the Apostles went upon an embassy that implied a new conception of man, such as before had entered no man's mind. Without distinction of race or sex or estate, men were to be taught that God was their Father, and were to express in a visible symbol the washing away of the old and the resurrection of the new humanity. The exalted idea of man that went out from Judæa to change the institutions of men was alone sufficient to reconstruct society and inaugurate a new epoch in the history of the world.

1. (1) Spread throughout the civilized nations was a profound contempt for labor and the laborer. Cicero had said: "All who live by mercenary labor do a degrading business. No noble sentiment can come from a workshop." The wise Seneca, one of the much-lauded Stoics, had taught: "The invention of the arts belongs to the vilest slaves. Wisdom dwells in loftier regions; she soils not her hands with labor." None but slaves engaged in any form of toil. Pauperism was widespread among the people. Under Augustus two hundred thousand persons were fed from the public granaries of Rome. Among such idlers, who claimed indolence as an hereditary and inalienable right, Paul went to live and to earn his bread by manual labor. Writing to the Corinthians he says: "We labor, working with our own hands."

And to the Thessalonians: "If any would not work, neither should he eat." The agitators of our day plead for the "rights" of labor. The disciples of that day were taught the "duty" of labor. In the "Apostolic Constitutions," Clement is reported as writing, "Labor according to your estate in all sanctity, in order that you may be able to succor your unfortunate brethren and that you may not be a charge to the church. We ourselves, who preach the word of the gospel, do not neglect labor of another order. Among us, some are fishers, others artisans, others husbandmen. We are never idle." Is it a wonder that in three centuries these heroic Christians, led by such devoted leaders, even amid violent persecutions and subjected to cruel taxation, rose to wealth and power in the Roman Empire and won for themselves the first places in the nation? Ignatius, Justin, and Epiphanius give similar testimony to the industry of the disciples of Christ and exhort their brethren to emulate their example.[1]

2) Thus dignified and rendered honorable by Christian practice, labor received a veritable "rehabilitation." The fourth Council of Carthage solemnly decreed that "it was good that every clerk win his bread either by trade or by cultivating the ground."[2] In addition to their literary studies, all candidates for orders were required to learn a trade. Augustine stirred his generation by his famous treatise "On the

---

[1] Const. Apost. ii, 67; Ignatius, Epist. vii, ad Tarsenes; Justin, De Vita Christiana; Epiphanius, Heres, lxxx.
[2] Concil. Carthag. li, lii, liii.

Work of Monks," in which he demanded that none should be idle. Benedict intermingled labor with prayer, and the Benedictine order required seven hours of daily toil, four hours of which must be spent in manual labor. These monks wandered to every land, true missionaries of industry, and at last Europe was transformed from a country of idlers and paupers into a busy scene of honorable labor. The origin of the great corporations of workmen is still obscure. Some have professed to find traces of them in the capitularies of Charlemagne. It is certain, however, that they grew up under the influence of Christian teaching and laid the foundations of organized industry throughout the world.[3]

(3) From its very inception Christianity began in the most effective way to undermine the almost universal system of human slavery. To have opposed it directly and radically, in the circumstances that then existed, would have been to suppress Christianity itself; but what the ultimate effect of Christianity must be is discernible in Paul's course with Onesimus, as related in his beautiful and pathetic letter to Philemon. That Paul was sensible of the dreadful curse of slavery there can be no doubt. "For public depravity to reach its utmost depths of degradation," says a French writer on slavery, "there needed to be a being with the passions and attractions of a man, yet stripped by public opinion of all the moral obligations of a human being; all whose wildest excesses

---

[3] For the history of guilds, religious, social, and industrial, see George Howell's The Conflicts of Capital and Labor, chap. i.

were lawful, provided they were commanded by a master. Such a being was the Roman slave."[4] But such a being could not long exist under Christian influence. Almost immediately amelioration was introduced into the slave's condition, enfranchisement usually followed among Christian slaveholders, innumerable death-bed liberations marked the effect of Christian tendencies, the moral sense was gradually stirred to perception, and slavery has finally vanished from the earth in every Christian land. It was morally impossible that the relation of owner and chattel could permanently continue between Christian brethren.

(4) Christianity not only gradually liberated labor from its yoke of bondage, but rendered it conscientious even to consecration. "Labor in all sanctity," says Clement, and the Christian workman began to sanctify his toil. The builders of the great cathedrals have left us examples of this sanctified workmanship. Not only those marvels of human construction themselves, but the holy inspiration that toiled upon them, has Christianity given to the world. "The architectural investigator of the nineteenth century is amazed and awed," says Brace, "to discover sometimes on remote portions of a church of the thirteenth century beautifully carved stonework, with every detail perfect, which no human eye has seen for six hundred years, as if the workman had chiseled these exquisite ornamentations 'for the love of God,' and not for the praise or hire of men. Nor does it lower the aspi-

---

[4] Wallon, quoted by Charles Loring Brace in Gesta Christi, chap. v.

ration that, once imbued with the devotion of the age, the architect and builder did his work not conscious always of the divine, but from the habit of honest and reverent work taught him by his faith. It was simply unconscious religion in practical life."[5]

2. The pagan love of wealth was based on the idea that happiness consists in selfish luxury. That conception was almost universal before the time of Christ and long afterward among those who did not accept his teaching. It is still the world's idea, except among Christian people. Aristotle said: "The title of citizen belongs only to those who need not work to live."[6] In the ancient state, property made the citizen. Without it a man fell into contempt and was treated as an outcast, or practically sold himself to men of wealth and power and became their political tool.

(1) The doctrine of Christ assumes the inherent worth and dignity of human nature, without regard to its externals. Neither wealth nor poverty makes a man greater or better in the sight of God. But a different idea is sometimes attributed to Christ. He is represented as totally condemning both riches and rich men. It would be difficult to show that either wealth itself or the accumulation of it is condemned by Christ. There are considerations that might even lead us to believe that he himself, in spite of the traditional view, was not wholly destitute. His saying, "The foxes have holes and the birds of the air

[5] Brace's Gesta Christi, p. 495.
[6] Aristotle's Politics, iii, 3, 2.

have nests, but the Son of man hath not where to lay his head," was spoken in view of his approaching passion and has obvious reference to his having no place of shelter from pursuit. It was the answer to a "certain scribe," who had proposed, not to live with him in his home, but to follow him as a disciple. It was like his reply to the mother of Zebedee's children, when he asked if they could endure his baptism. There is no ground, therefore, for the inference that Christ was absolutely homeless and penniless. Is it impossible that out of his thirty years of life before the beginning of his ministry, Jesus had gathered enough to furnish a home for his widowed mother? If Paul thought it becoming that he should supply his own necessities with the labor of his hands, is it probable that Jesus was for three years an absolute pensioner on public charity? His tender remembrance of his mother in his dying agony, when he transferred his filial duties to his loving disciple John, with the words, "Woman, behold, thy son," seems to imply a previous discharge of those duties by himself during all the years of his ministry. And the reported words of Jesus do not convince us of his antipathy to wealth. He does not censure prudent accumulation when he says, "Lay not up for yourselves treasures upon the earth," but selfish accumulation, laying up treasures for "yourselves," and laying them up upon the earth alone, instead of laying them up in heaven. "Labor not for the meat that perisheth" is not a prohibition of eating, or of acquiring food by labor, but of losing all thought of the lasting in toiling for the perishable. These are, indeed, dissuasions from the pursuit of wealth as the chief good, as the pagan world considered it, but not condemnations of wealth or its acquisition. The dangers of wealth are, however, made apparent. "Ye cannot serve God and Mammon." "How hardly shall they that have riches enter into the kingdom of God!" The difficulty is emphasized, but the impossibility is not asserted. "Woe unto you that are rich!" But if we ask wherefore, the answer runs, "For ye have received your consolation," — you have chosen a good that has consolation only for the present and have nothing for the future; you have made a woeful choice. The evil of it Paul explains: "They that will be rich fall into temptation and a snare, and into many foolish and hurtful lusts which drown men in destruction and perdition." It is not "money" but the "love" of it, the misplacement of affection belonging normally to nobler things, that is the "root of all evil." It is in "coveting after it" that some "have erred from the faith, and pierced themselves through with many sorrows."

(2) Paganism said, Love wealth; Christianity said, Love men. The contrast is beautifully exhibited in the new idea of wealth which Christ introduced into the world. "A man's life consisteth not in the abundance of the things which he possesseth," said Jesus. The world has usually thought that it does. Christ has led many millions to think otherwise. The power of the new doctrine is seen in the immediate

consequences of its acceptance. Of the church in Jerusalem we read : " And the multitude of them that believed were of one heart and of one soul; neither said any of them that aught of the things which he possessed was his own; but they had all things in common." In ever-widening circles the great wave of charity has spread throughout the world. The consecration of wealth to the good of man was a wholly new idea. These words of the Apostolic Constitutions seem like the very charter of Christian charity : " To orphans take the place of a father; to widows give the protection they would have had from their husbands; help young people who desire to marry with your counsels; find work for artisans; have pity on the infirm; receive strangers beneath your roof; give food and drink to those who are hungry and thirsty, and clothes to the naked; visit the sick and help the prisoners."[7] And note how wisely these duties are imposed. The absolutely helpless alone are to be provided for; the young and capable are to be put in the way of self-help; the accidentally unfortunate are to have their immediate needs supplied. Here is no indiscriminate and broadcast sacrifice of the rich to the poor. The whole movement is prompted by the recognition of the man, rather than the regard of circumstances; everything is designed to elevate, to comfort, to reform, or to assist the man and to make him master his surroundings and rise superior to his miseries. If charity sometimes manifested more of sympathy

[7] Const. Apost. iv, 2.

than of discernment, we must account it a phenomenon very rare in the world and too creditable to the faith of enthusiasts to deserve severe censure. It is true that the Church of Rome alone supported more then fifteen hundred poor people, and the Church at Antioch, in the time of Chrysostom, maintained more than three thousand. It is true that men like Basil the Great, and Paulinus of Nola, and Hilary of Arles, gave their entire estates to the poor, and that priests sold their sacerdotal robes, aye, even the golden vessels of the holy communion, in order to feed the poor. A more discriminating sympathy established homes for widows and orphans, hospitals for the sick and maimed, and asylums for abandoned women.[8]

(3) It has sometimes been thought that Christianity instituted and favored communistic life and denied the right of private property. This has been argued from the practice of the church at Jerusalem and the expressions of the early Christian Fathers. In the church at Jerusalem there was neither an authoritative community of goods nor was it intended for a model. It was a temporary expediency for meeting an emergency, when many of the disciples were poor, when sympathy drew all hearts together, and when union was essential to safety. The gifts were all voluntary. Ananias was not rebuked for retaining a part of his possessions, and his right to do this was expressly conceded. " Whiles it remained, *was it not thine own?* and after it was

---

[8] C. Schmidt's The Social Results of Early Christianity, book ii, chap. v.

sold, was it not in thine own power? Why hast thou conceived this thing in thy heart? Thou hast not lied unto men, but unto God." And throughout the whole thrilling narrative there is no slightest intimation that the right of property was brought in question. It has been affirmed that the Fathers openly and strongly deny the right of private possession. Their words do, indeed, seem to imply this.[9] Basil, Chrysostom, Jerome, Ambrose, and Clement all employ language that sounds communistic; and yet I feel confident that, however revolutionary single sentences may sound when abstracted from their setting, they were intended as merely rhetorical appeals to practical charity or the high colors in pictures of an ideal state. Clement of Alexandria wrote a special treatise to prove that "poverty is not essential to salvation, that riches are not a reason for exclusion from the kingdom of God, and that it would be irrational to suppose that Christianity demands the renunciation of property, because in that case beggars would be the best of the faithful, which is contradicted by experience." [10]

[9] As examples of the apparently communistic utterances of the Christian Fathers, take the following: —
"The rich man is a thief." — Saint Basil. "The rich are robbers; a kind of equality must be effected by making gifts out of their abundance. Better all things were in common." — Saint Chrysostom. "Opulence is always the product of theft, committed, if not by the actual possessor, by his ancestors." — Saint Jerome. "Nature created community; private property is the offspring of usurpation." — Saint Ambrose. "In strict justice, everything should belong to all. Iniquity alone has created private property." — Saint Clement. Quoted from Bossuet by Laveleye in The Socialism of To-day, introduction. But see the references below.

[10] Quis Dives Salvetur, vol. ii, p. 935, of the writings of Clement. See also the references cited by Schmidt, op. cit., where Augustine, Ambrose,

Christianity taught mankind to endure poverty without despair, and to possess riches without sensuality and pride. It has taught the needy not to envy the rich, and the wealthy not to oppress the poor. It has done more than any other influence that ever touched the life of man to obliterate those class-distinctions which create strife and bitterness in the human heart, and have made discord and misery where peace and happiness should reign.

3. (1) Without doubt no single cause so undermined and disturbed the welfare of ancient society as the relations between the sexes that paganism developed and fostered. Marriage, before Christianity modified the life of woman and the opinion in which she was universally held, was considered a necessary evil, whose end was the gratification of passion and the perpetuation of the state. It had fallen into such discredit that celibacy had to be heavily taxed, in order to sustain the growth of population; and illicit relations had rendered exceptional the chastity of men and almost universal the debasement of women. In Rome the home had ceased to exist. Woman was a helpless dependent either under her father's care or her husband's power. Her only hope of freedom lay either in the life of a courtesan or in those "free marriages," enduring at the option of the parties, which custom had made the most common kind in Rome. Given in marriage without her consent, expelled from her

---

Jerome, Paulinus of Nola, and many other writers of the early Church teach that riches are not to be condemned in themselves, chap. v.

husband's house upon the slightest pretext, deprived of partnership in his wealth, under the tutelage of his male relatives, without other education than that derived by contact with her family, the companion of eunuchs and female slaves, confined to the house as to a prison, treated as a ministrant to lust and passion, valued only as the necessary agent for the perpetuation of the race, timorous or frivolous or tyrannical as her circumstances made her, with no attractions but those of nature, inevitably lost with nature's decay, without love and respect, — the pagan woman was an object so pitiable that it was often thought a mercy to destroy her life in infancy. It is the voice of pagan antiquity, rather than the individual censor Metellus Numidius, that utters the words which he pronounced before the assembled people: "If nature had allowed us to be without women, we should have been relieved of very troublesome companions." [11]

(2) It is sometimes thought that the increased respect for women, the elevation of conjugal affection, and the higher standard of personal purity which the subsequent centuries reveal, are attributable to that chastity and esteem for the gentler sex which Tacitus and others discovered and praised among the Germanic races. A very moderate degree of virtue might easily excite the astonishment of a Roman in the age of Tacitus. A high degree of personal devotion may well be accorded to German women, but polygamy was not unknown among

[11] Quoted by Aulus Gellius, Opera, i, 6.

the early Germans, the jealousy and tyranny of husbands often amounted to absolute cruelty, and woman in Germany was and has been ever since, with some modifications through Christian influence, the faithful slave of man. Wives were bought and adultery was compounded by the purchase of another wife. Brutality was common in the treatment of women, and even to-day the bearing of burdens, subjection to the husband, and physical punishment for conjugal offences continue to be customary in Germany more conspicuously than in other lands.[12]

(3) But it was impossible that the being who had borne the world a Saviour could continue to be despised and cruelly treated by those who loved and trusted him. The Blessed Virgin became a holy image in the eyes of the Christian world. The doctrines of Christ made no distinction of sex. All were equal before God. Even more responsively than man's, the loving heart of woman turned to the warmth and light of the gospel. Oppressed and overburdened, despised and spurned, the fine sensibilities and large capacities of affection, that centuries of degradation had not destroyed, awoke to a flame of sincere love and adoration, and the disciples of Christ included more women than men. Not only the high ideal of purity, the rigid laws of divorce, and the tender regard for children, all claiming a divine authority, but the sweet spiritual companionship strengthened and perfected the conjugal tie.

[12] For the position of woman under the Germanic tribes, see the full treatment in chapter xi of Brace's Gesta Christi.

For the first time, souls, immortal in their union, were wedded. Marriage was no longer looked upon as a social function merely, as it is in a state of nature. It typified the union of Christ and his pure bride, the Church. It was celebrated at the altar with the benediction of Christ's minister, it opened new fountains of intercourse and sympathy, it created the home with its Bible and its daily prayers, it spread a table upon which God's blessing was invoked to rest, it demanded faithfulness and devotion and propriety and gentleness, it was indissoluble in its nature, it led to companionship in the endless ages of a coming life, it found its fruition in immortal beings and holy hopes by the birth of children. Never upon the earth did a more stupendous change take place in human society, than when the first Christian bridegroom led the first Christian bride to the altar, touching her hand and gazing upon her face, as if they might be the holy habitation of the Mother of God herself!

4. (1) It is evident that Christianity places a high value upon childhood. The love of children was a Hebrew virtue. But the whole spirit of Christianity dignifies and exalts the child. The affections awakened in the hearts of Christian parents, the beautiful images presented by the history of the Saviour's own nativity, the touching picture of his blessing little children, his expressed desire that they might be suffered to come to him, and his requirement in believers of childlike docility and trustfulness, all combined to deepen and refine the regard for chil-

dren. The rights of childhood found recognition with the introduction of Christianity. The paternal power had before allowed the father unlimited authority over his child, including the right to expose him to death at birth, to sell him as a slave, and to take his life. The weak and the superfluous children, and especially the girls, were often abandoned in this manner. Whoever found the child might retain it and rear it as a slave. If sound in body, this was usually its fate. A curious revelation of the inconsistency of men is found in the fact that the famous words of Terence, which evoked thunders of applause from the Roman audience that listened to his play, — "I am a man; nothing pertaining to man do I think foreign from me," — are contained in a comedy whose plot turns upon the survival of an infant daughter commanded to be exposed to death by the very man who uttered this sentence.[13]

(2) The education of children was not neglected by antiquity, but it was by no means universal. The most careful education was found among the Hebrews. Greek education aimed at æsthetic culture, but confined it entirely to the few, mostly excluding women and slaves, who made up most of the population. Roman education was likewise restricted and had no higher ideal than fitness for political citizenship. "The education of paganism,"

---

[13] See the Heauton-timorumenos of Terence. The line "Homo sum; humani nihil a me alienum puto," according to Augustine, moved the whole audience — though many of the spectators were rude and ignorant — to thunders of applause.

says an able historian of education, "was imperfect. It was controlled by wrong principles and confined within too narrow limits. It did not grasp the worth of the individual in its fullness. It never freed itself from the narrowness of national character. . . . But with the advent of Christ into the world, there came a new era in history."[14] Dr. William T. Harris, speaking of this subject, says: "The influence of such an idea as that of the divine-human God condescending to assume the sorrows and trials of mortal life, all for the sake of the elevation of individual souls, the humblest and weakest as well as the mightiest and most exalted, is potent to transform civilization."[15] Henceforth, the life of a child is valued as a precious treasure, and the shaping of its destiny is the noblest work of man.

(3) The Roman Empire enjoyed an organized system of public schools, founded by the emperors, and endowed by such statesmen as Hadrian, Marcus Aurelius, Vespasian, and Theodosius. They extended throughout all the cities of the empire. The early Christians availed themselves of them; but as they were intended to impart an education whose end was the State, and as their studies consisted mainly in the reading of pagan authors, schools of catechumens were founded to prepare candidates for baptism. With the invasion of the Franks, the imperial schools were closed. After an interval during which there seems to have been little but domestic instruc-

---

[14] F. V. N. Painter's History of Education, chap. iii.
[15] See the preface to the work last cited.

tion, the Church instituted an educational revival. The Church councils from the sixth century on to the time of Charlemagne repeatedly urge the establishment of parish and monastic schools, which seem to have been opened in great numbers. The palace-school of Charlemagne in which the great Alcuin taught, and others founded under his direction, are well known in history. The foundations of the great universities were at length laid by the Church. The imperfection of all these educational efforts we cannot fail to recognize, but we must not forget the world's indebtedness to them. Christianity, as such, has never antagonized learning, but has proved its most faithful guardian. Besides the conservation of such knowledge as the ancient world possessed, Christianity has contributed an element wholly new in the training of the young. It has impressed upon men the value of the individual and striven to secure his perfection of himself by the development of character and the pursuit of moral ideals. It has also trained the human mind to habits of introspection and self-analysis that lie at the basis of all true philosophy and without which the scientific spirit itself would possess neither form nor impulse.

5. The moral and intellectual changes of a people soon show themselves in legislation. Even under the pagan emperors, Christianity began its ameliorating and elevating influence upon the laws. The subject presents too many details for our narrow limits, but deserves a special study in such works as " Gesta Christi," by Charles Loring Brace, and " The

Social Results of Early Christianity," by Professor Schmidt, of Strasburg, with their extensive references to authorities. I can simply enumerate a few of the most significant of these moral victories in the field of legislation.

(1) The earliest and most important effect was upon personal status. Constantine removed the paternal power of life and death and rendered the killing of a child a crime equal to parricide. He also extended the son's rights of property. Julian forbade immoderate penalties to be inflicted upon children. Daughters were endowed with heirship. Divorce was restricted to a few causes, as when a husband is a murderer, a magician, or a violator of tombs, or the wife an adulteress or guilty of evil practices. Civil equality was established between husband and wife, and adultery was punished with death. Chastity was required by the laws of Justinian, though he weakened again the legislation on divorce. The unnatural vices so frequent in antiquity that Cicero said it was a disgrace not to indulge in them, vices unnamed and unknown in the modern Christian world, were severely punished under Theodosius. Numerous ameliorations were introduced into the life of the slave. To poison or throw him to wild beasts was made homicide. Liberty was declared inalienable, so that no free child could become a slave. The marriage relation between slaves was regarded as indissoluble by separation. Every facility for liberating slaves became the policy of the law. Under Basil (867) the slaves of a master whose

property reverted to the State became free; for so ran the law: "It would be an outrage to the holiness of God, to the wisdom of the prince, and to the conscience of man, not to permit the death of the master to break the yoke of servitude."[16]

(2) The laws relating to personal conduct were equally revolutionized. The stranger, who had always been considered an enemy by the German tribes before their conversion, the wrecked at sea, who had been regarded as legitimate prey, and whose vessels were sometimes lured to destruction upon the rocks for the sake of booty, were brought within the protection of justice. Private feuds, which had raged from generation to generation, requiring the avenging of blood by a member of the family, were commuted by payments of money or adjusted by judicial tribunals. "The Peace of God" waved the white flag of truce over bloody battlefields and called the combatants to the silent hush of prayer. Earlier than this the horrible conflicts of the gladiators had been brought to a termination. Honorius vainly tried to stop these inhuman shows by the degradation of the gladiatorial profession. At last (404) an eastern monk, Telemachus, crossed the seas, and at Rome threw himself into the arena between the swords of the contestants. The fury of the crowd demanded his immediate death, but his blood was the last that flowed from human veins in that Flavian amphithea-

---

[16] A very discriminating and compendious estimate of the influence of Christianity upon Roman legislation may be found in Morey's Outlines of Roman Law, period iv, chap. ii.

tre, whose silent, crumbling walls stand as a monument to this fearless martyr. An imperial edict suppressed this cruel sport forever.[17]

6. We can barely mention the amelioration of punishment that Christianity has introduced. "No classic legislator, so far as we can recall," says Brace, "had ever cared for that unfortunate class — the prisoners." Prison reform began under Constantine. The accused were to be examined without delay, they were to be treated in a humane manner, persons under arrest were not to be tortured, and prisons were required to have air and light. Paul's confinement in that gloomy, subterranean Mamertine prison at Rome may have been, in part, in its results, vicarious suffering for the accused of the future. In all of this was that exalted view of man which Christ had taught, and God's image was not to be marred. "Let those who are condemned," reads a sentence of Constantine's, "not be branded on the forehead, that the majesty of the face formed in the image of celestial beauty be not dishonored."[18] But the glory of Christianity is not shown in prison reform, ancient or modern, though it is great, so much as in the changed theory of all punitive treatment. The reform and salvation of the criminal are aims exclusively Christian in their origin. If the sentiment of our age has adopted them as its ideals in punishment, it is because of that latent and unconscious Christianity that is working like leaven in the hearts

---

[17] Theodoret, Historia Ecclesiastica, v, 26.
[18] Codex Theodosii, liber xv, title 8, 1.

of men, even while their lips are framing a denial of its presence.

We cannot linger longer to recount what Christianity has done for society. If any think that much of our social progress can be attributed to other causes, a survey of the non-Christian world will dispel that illusion. Wherever Christian influence has not penetrated, the pre-Christian social conditions still exist. Something depends upon natural temperament, indeed, in the reformation of racial characteristics, and few vices or defects of social life are universal. But nowhere is there a true conception of human worth and dignity, where Christ's teachings have not been felt. A contempt for labor, with its accompaniment of human servitude; the regard of caste and class-distinctions, with violent contrasts of wealth and poverty unmodified by pity and charity; the degradation of woman and disregard of personal chastity; the indifference to children and their continuance in ignorance and vice; the inequality of legislation and the dominion of personal hate and cruel revenge, — these are the social phenomena with which we expect to meet whenever we overstep the boundaries of Christian lands and enter the regions where the life and doctrines of Jesus are unknown.

That his power is not greater than it is among ourselves is testimony to the magnitude of the work his teaching has accomplished in the world; for it has met with the same and even greater obstacles, and yet it has triumphantly surmounted them in its steady but not unimpeded progress. When we consider how, in these centuries, it has changed the life and institutions of society; how it has given labor a rehabilitation, consecrated wealth to human benefit, honored and ennobled woman, crowned the head of childhood with the coronet of love and knowledge, swept away traces of barbarism from the codes of law and tempered them with justice and mercy, let sunlight and hope into the cells of the prison and broken the fetters of the slave, — may we not look for its solution of the passing problems of the present, for its Author has said: "Lo, I am with you alway, even unto the end of the world"?

III.

CHRISTIANITY AND THE PROBLEMS OF LABOR.

CHRISTIANITY AND THE PROBLEMS OF LABOR.

I. THE EVOLUTION OF INDUSTRY.
    1. Eras of Industrial Progress:
        (1) The Era of Hunting;
        (2) The Era of Cattle Raising;
        (3) The Era of Agriculture;
        (4) The Era of the Mechanic Arts.
    2. The Correlation of Wants and Wealth.
    3. The Causes of Wealth and Labor.
    4. Progressive and Improgressive Labor.
    5. The Division of Labor.
    6. The Invention of Machinery.

II. THE CONTEMPORARY PROBLEMS OF LABOR.
    1. The Problem of Increasing Wealth.
        (1) Is the Increase of Wealth Desirable?
        (2) Wealth but a Means to Life as an End.
        (3) The Increase of the Laborer's Productivity.
        (4) The Avoidance of Waste.
    2. The Problem of the Laborer's Rights.
        (1) The Foundation of Human Rights.
        (2) The Right to Self and One's Powers.
        (3) The Right to the Product of One's Powers.
        (4) Wealth as a Social Product.
        (5) The Ground of Taxation.
        (6) The Right of Property.
        (7) The Right of Property in Land.
        (8) The Universal Stewardship.

III.

CHRISTIANITY AND THE PROBLEMS OF LABOR.

I.

1. THE first problem of society is that of subsistence, or the production of those commodities that contribute to life. The first cry of every human being is the bitter wail of hunger. But, as for each individual added to our race provision is made, without his own exertion, for the satisfaction of his earliest needs, so also it was in the infancy of humanity for the first wants of our species. Originating, probably, in some fertile and temperate region of southern Asia, the first men were able to satisfy their hunger with the spontaneous fruits of the generous earth, and a genial sky rendered superfluous both clothing and habitations. I know not how great progress in the tilling of the earth the biblical narrative intends to ascribe to the Adam of Genesis, but its own subsequent account of the origin of metallurgy justifies our belief that the Edenic implements were of a very primitive character.

(1) In the course of the migration and dispersion of men, in which the command to "multiply and replenish the earth" was executed, impinging of the population upon the food-supply, as well as the rigors

of more severe climates, involved the use of the flesh of animals for food and of their skins for clothing, while caves in the earth, natural or artificial, afforded the protection of dwellings. Thus men found themselves existing in the era of hunting.

(2) The perception of the waste involved and the uncertainty of a sufficient supply, when animals were killed at random in a wild state, must early have suggested their domestication, and we may picture to ourselves the patriarchal family with its flocks and herds roaming over the pasture-lands, subsisting principally upon the fatlings of the flocks and dwelling in the movable tents adapted to the nomadic life of the era of cattle-raising.

(3) Again, the physical requirements of the growth of population, coupled with contentions arising concerning the occupation of the soil, like that reported between Abraham and Lot, ultimately introduced the permanent demarkation of the land into separate holdings, and the establishment of villages for residence. This necessitated the cultivation of the more limited apportionment of the soil, in order to produce by art what was not afforded by nature, and thus began the agricultural era.

(4) Finally, the exigencies of defence against the encroachment of hostile neighbors, together with the demand for agricultural implements, required the equipment of armies, the erection of walled towns for refuge, the construction of engines of war and the working of metals, with its attendant division of labor and organization of military, civil, and political

institutions, which characterize the era of mechanic arts. The arts thus rendered necessary, after remaining for centuries subsidiary to the ends which first called them into being, have at last been brought to minister directly and chiefly to the desires of the people; the militant spirit has become secondary to the industrial, and the principal trait of contemporary society is the industrialism that creates its enormous wealth and whose interests evoke its highest solicitude.

2. Civilization begins in man's needs and is meant to afford him satisfaction. He is never quite satisfied, and yet he is not of necessity unhappy in any stage of his industrial progress. The growth of his wants is correlated to the increase of his wealth. The sight of wealth produces new wants. The Pacific Islanders are not dissatisfied with life. Contact with civilized men, however, often generates in them new desires and material civilization moves along this line of new wants created by the desire of new wealth.

It is universally conceded that men were never in the history of the world so well supplied with commodities of every kind as they are to-day. The fact is capable of statistical proof, but it is too apparent to require the time and trouble.[1] The cause of the present industrial discontent is the confrontation of wealth and poverty, with its startling contrast of

---

[1] For the statistical proof of this statement see Giffen's Progress of the Working Classes, pp. 5, 26; Stebbin's Progress from Poverty, pp. 7, 9, and pp. 30, 33; and Mulhall's History of Prices, pp. 130, 133.

luxury on the one side and misery on the other. Men who work as common laborers to-day enjoy more of the physical comforts of life than the men and women who landed on Plymouth Rock. They are not so happy or so contented, and the reason is that they think they have not their fair proportion of wealth.

3. The ultimate cause of wealth is labor, in its wide sense of human activity for the satisfaction of wants. This is an economic commonplace. But the economists seldom discuss the question, What is the cause of labor? Mallock says it is the desire for social inequality.[2] This is a true but not a complete answer. Men labor primarily to sustain existence. When they have the means of doing this, they cease from labor, unless they have an additional impulse. They have this in the desire of social inequality. They see others enjoying more than themselves. They desire to rise into the superior class. This desire renders them industrious and economical. By more exertion and less immediate indulgence they hope to arrive at a superior condition. Progress has followed this line. It results in the acquisition of commodities and possessions that elevate one's estate. Such accumulations are "capital," because they are not only the products of the "head" (*caput*), but constitute a "head," or source, of further advantage.

4. If we ask in what manner capital is produced, we find that it is not simply the product of labor, but

[2] Mallock's Social Equality, chap. iv.

of a particular kind of labor. There is labor which is wholly improgressive, whose whole result is necessary for the subsistence of the worker. A man who employs the whole day hunting his dinner with a bow and arrow in the forest never acquires any capital. He consumes the product of his day's labor and in the morning must resume his hunting. But there is another kind of labor. It is progressive. The man who invents a trap may catch every day what will last for two days. He may give away the subsistence of one day to another man who is willing to use the time for his service. All capital is the result of this kind of labor. It requires some skill. The more skilful it is, the more capital it will produce. A man with a very fertile brain devises ways to obtain in one day the food for many days. This gives him command over as many men who are capable only of improgressive labor as he can feed. They would as soon serve him as to hunt food. If he assures them subsistence in advance and with certainty, they will probably prefer the certainty of subsistence from him to the uncertainty of subsistence without him. His knowledge and enterprise make him a master.

Looking back over human history we are compelled to refer all industrial progress and all increase of wealth to such enterprise and knowledge. Civilization has been rendered possible through the improvement of men. Universal ignorance gives us savagery, idleness, and famine. Intelligent chiefs give us barbarism, slavery, and poverty. An educated class gives us civilization, free labor, and plenty.

Educated masses give us enlightenment, organized labor, and abundance. Universal education will give us refinement, intellectualized labor, and wealth. If we examine these superimposed planes of social existence we shall see that the elevation of man has increased wealth; that the ascent of man has produced the multiplication of his possessions; that a condition of ignorance is a state in which the mind values *things* only, and that a condition of universal education is a state in which the chief value is placed on *man*. I infer, therefore, that the influence that has done most to emphasize the value of man and afford an elevated conception of his nature, is the influence that has done most to create the wealth of the world. That influence, we have already seen, is the influence of Jesus. I take it to be a principal cause of the world's wealth. The conclusion is justified by the fact that the wealthiest nations of the earth are the Christian nations. This leads me to think that Christianity has an important relation to the problems of labor.

5. A principal cause of wealth is the division of labor. It is based on the variation of aptitude and ability to accomplish results and the apportionment of tasks to those adapted to them. Its beginnings are too remote for discovery, but we may readily imagine them in the first human family. Man would naturally undertake the heavier and more active work of securing food. Woman would assume the lighter task of its preparation, in conjunction with the maternal care of children. But our knowledge of

savage life does not warrant this natural assumption. Among the savage peoples we invariably find the whole burden of labor thrown upon woman, the least qualified to bear it, while man spends his days in idle enjoyment. When the plane of existence is reached where more labor is necessary, in order to supply a greater number of wants, we find that those who labor are again not the strongest, but the weakest, the slaves, whose inferior powers render them the more easily reduced to subjection. If we examine history, so far as it throws light upon the subject, we discover everywhere the same abnormal phenomenon — the strong idle, and the weak compelled to labor. The only exception is met when we reach those times and those lands where the influence of Christ has been felt. There we find labor accounted honorable, woman more generally released from the burdens of toil, slaves progressively liberated from servitude, and strong, free men voluntarily joining in the "rehabilitation of labor." But compulsory labor is the least progressive and the least enterprising kind. All truly progressive labor is free. Accordingly, we find the lands and times that have endured the curse of slavery suffering also from the curse of poverty. From this, also, I infer that the influence of Jesus is a vital element in the labor and industrial life of the world.

6. Another factor in the production of wealth is the improvement of tools, the invention of machines, and the application of natural forces to production or invention. It creates at one stroke a power that

is equivalent to a thousand men. It extends the emancipation of the slave by freeing men from the slavery of muscular toil. It multiplies the commodities of life until those that in former days were the luxuries of the few become the universal possessions of the people. This is the result of progressive, not at all of improgressive, labor. It gives to every one, who has anything to buy with, an unearned increment for his money too great for estimation. We read of the "unearned increment of land" and of the "unearned increment of capital." There is also an immense "unearned increment of labor." I do not say that all the inventions of our modern era were conceived with the sole purpose of lightening the burdens of men, but it is an incontestable fact that thousands of them have originated from the desire that a difficult and wearisome work might be made easier. It can, however, be justly maintained that inventions would be wholly without motive of any kind under conditions of slavery. The master has never cared to apply his intelligence for lightening the burden of slaves, and the slave could not thus lighten his burden. The psychology of progress explains the history of progress. If non-Christian lands have produced no labor-saving machinery, it is because oppression did not care, and servitude had not the power, to lighten human toil. For this reason, again, I affirm that the influence of Jesus is the life of industry.

II.

There are two contemporary problems of labor that deserve our consideration. They are the problem of increasing wealth and the problem of the laborer's rights.

1. Is it desirable to continue the increase of wealth and how can it be increased, if desirable? (1) The acquisitive faculty in man does not hesitate to answer the first part of this double question in the affirmative. Yes, wealth is good, men generally respond. And what has Christianity to say? Is it possible that Christianity can be a principal cause in the production of wealth, as we have shown it to be, and at the same time censure that increase? Undoubtedly Christ rebukes rich men for their greed; and reminds them that material wealth is not the highest good, but does he anywhere condemn the multiplication of commodities to be used for the wellbeing of man? I have failed to find in his doctrines any such condemnation. On the contrary, it is everywhere assumed by him that material goods are really good. Lazarus was in pitiable lack of them, and Dives had the full enjoyment of them, and Christ recognizes the fact that the condition of Dives was a more desirable condition than that of Lazarus, apart from the moral qualities and relations of the two men. The shame of the contrast was that Lazarus lacked while Dives was without compassion. If one may be "diligent in business," and at the same time "serving the Lord," the fruits of diligence cannot

be morally undesirable. It is impossible for men to develop their higher powers, to find opportunity for self-improvement, to realize the conditions of health and beneficence, without the possession of some measure of wealth. Wealth, then, is good, its increase is desirable, from a Christian point of view.

(2) But there is an important limitation of this truth. Wealth is a means, not an end. The whole truth is expressed in the words of Christ : " A man's life consisteth not in the abundance of the things that he possesseth." The really wealthy man is not the man who has most, but the man who can use most, who can make things most subsidiary to his life, who most completely realizes his own and other's weal. Christ enlarges, ennobles, and transfigures the conception of wealth. The lower conception excludes all that is noblest, by excluding all that is really human. Possession is a graded and an evanescent power. The barn-builder of Christ's parable never completed his granaries. No matter what material transformation it undergoes, wealth can never be preserved unless it contributes to life. The sooner it does so the better. Not necessarily to be immediately consumed, but to be made the instrument of life. A workshop or a library enters into life, if it be rightly placed, but a pile of unused gold is no better than a pile of unused stones. It may be riches, but it is not wealth. But neither is the workshop or the library wealth, unless skilful hands or active minds come into relation with them. There is the ring of Christ's own truth in Ruskin's words : " There is no wealth but life ; life,

with its powers of love, of joy, of admiration. That country is the richest which nourishes the greatest number of noble and happy human beings; that man is richest who, having perfected the functions of his own life to the utmost, has also the widest helpful influence, both personal and by means of his possessions, over the lives of others." [3]

(3) The increase of wealth is best realized by whatever increases the productivity of the laborer. Whatever lifts a man out of the sphere of improgressive labor and places him on the plane of progressive labor, increases wealth. It does it directly by enlarging his life, and indirectly by making him a creator of wealth. This idea is entering into the minds of business men as they ponder over these problems of labor. Says a recent writer on this subject, after a survey of the history of industry: "Labor must be treated at least as well as any other source of power. A steam-engine is well housed, well fed with fuel, well oiled, and well governed by a competent engineer. For its economic use, it must work smoothly and continuously. We must supply it with all that its material constitution requires. The economic use of the horse demands that he be well fed, well housed, and well treated. We must supply him with all that his physical nature demands for its healthy working. In like manner, the economic use of the man requires that all the conditions of his wellbeing shall be respected. His physical nature must be supported by good food, clean and comfortable hous-

---

[3] Ruskin's Unto This Last, Essay iv, Ad Valorem.

ing, and all other good sanitary conditions; but he has an intellectual being as well; its health must be provided for by education, by the literature, at least, of his business; for he is a moral power, sensitive to right and wrong. He must be influenced to right and withdrawn from wrong, or you will have a destroyer, not a worker. But is the economic ground the only one on which this equitable treatment of the laborer is necessary? Nay, this man is your brother."[4] I know a village in Pennsylvania, owned by a family of Christian men, where all these principles, and even more extended applications of them than is here suggested, have been in practice for years. The neat houses with their pretty gardens and flowers in the windows, with instruments of music in the spare-rooms, the neat schoolhouse and commodious church, have been built for the workmen upon a model plan. During a period when other factories of like kind were almost universally closed on account of low prices, this community went steadily on with its manufacture. No man left work on account of lowered wages, no time was lost, and at the end the goods were ready for the high market for which they had been reserved. Experience has in that establishment added its evidence to faith, that care for the workman brings its own reward. I need not add that the proprietors are Christian men and believe that Christian principles have relation to industrial problems.

[4] The Labor Problem, edited by W. E. Barnes, chap. ii, by J. A. Waterworth.

(4) Another element in the increase of wealth is the avoidance of waste. This opens a broad subject. It is impossible to treat it exhaustively. There is, first of all, the waste of war and its accessories. It is probably true that standing armies and navies are necessary in the present political condition of the world, and that the most certain way to preserve peace is to have well-trained soldiers and officers and implements of destruction so terrific that the mere thought of their destructiveness is sufficient to prevent their actual employment. But, at the same time, the cost of sustaining a nation on a war-footing is so enormous that it is a serious drainage on industry. First, vast numbers of men are abstracted from the ranks of labor to serve as soldiers and officers, and then, besides their support, the preparation of costly munitions of war is required of those who are left for actual production. Within the last thirty years the debts of the governments of Europe have increased nine billions of dollars. This is owing to four great wars which have had no connection with the rights or progress of man, but have been waged to maintain the "balance of power." The present aggregate debts are twenty billions. The armies and navies and interest on debts absorb fourteen hundred millions annually, of which only a fraction is necessary. The combined cost of civil service and education is about one fourth of the cost of this luxury of the "balance of power." This superfluity is an exaction of twenty-seven dollars from each laborer and of forty-five dollars from each family of five. In Italy

it abstracts fifty dollars, in England sixty-two dollars, and in France sixty-five dollars from each family. It is a cruel wrong. Christianity applied to practice would have saved it. It would have settled the wars by arbitration and capitalized their cost as public wealth. The United States presents the picture of a federation of commonwealths with greater territorial extent than that of Europe, without standing armies, and with a navy that is a mere jest. The civil war cost more than the purchase of the slaves would have required, to take no account of blood and suffering. The settlement of our claim against England by Christian methods is one of the triumphs of human history. Christianity would carry the same method into industrial warfare, the perpetual struggle that at once embitters and demoralizes men and impedes the creation of wealth. It declares that industry is not, in its ideal, a selfish struggle for existence, a desperate battle of landlord and tenant, of employer and employed, a conflict of interests that forever clash and tend to annihilate one another. It indicates how this problem of wealth-creation can be solved and the only method of solution. It says to arrogant landlordism, your true interest lies in having happy and prosperous tenants; to envious labor, your hope rests in a universal progress led by enterprise and sustained by capital; to mercenary capital, your security and permanence depend upon the activity of labor and the pacific participation of all in its rewards; to avaricious enterprise, your dreams of fortune can become realities only when large classes of men are able to enjoy your products. Therefore, cease the strife which, however it may end, must eventuate in some one's overthrow, and the emergence from the smoke of desolation of the more pathetic question, What shall society do with the vanquished?

2. Perhaps a deeper problem, and one more difficult to solve than that of increasing wealth, is the problem of the laborer's rights. (1) I say the "*laborer's* rights," because there are no "rights of *labor*." Rights belong only to persons, to men as moral beings. And whatever "rights" the laborer has, he has in virtue of his manhood, not in virtue of his labor. It is difficult to escape class distinctions and the idea of class privileges. Rights do not belong to classes, but to men. What is it in a man that entitles him to rights? It is the capacity for duty. He is a being whose nature has ends; it is his duty to realize those ends, and he is morally free to realize them. Suppose he does not. Then he does not realize his manhood. Manhood is not a mechanical product of nature. Nature furnishes capacities and faculties, but manhood is the self-determined product of the man himself. To realize manhood, one must be free. The essence of personality is freedom. Rights inhere in personality, because it is free, because it has duties, because it has an end to realize. This cannot be said of any creature lower than man. Such a creature is not an end, but a means. Its purpose of being is not realized in itself. Man is lord over the lower creatures; bound, no

doubt, to exercise his lordship in a truly lordly way, in a way comporting with his rational nature and not like a brute, but still possessed of dominion. The animal world exists for him, is for his service, and finds its end in him, not in itself. Man, too, is under the dominion of a Superior, but his end is to become like him, to realize in his own person the spiritual excellence of God.

(2) If rights inhere in a man, what rights has he? The right to realize himself, to attain the ends of his being. This is, with relation to himself, his duty. With relation to others, it is his right. He has a right, therefore, to himself and to the unrestricted exercise of his natural powers. He cannot rightly be enslaved. To enslave him is to disregard this right and to render impossible this duty. If it should be said that another man or a society of men has a right to a man, on what ground could this right be defended? On what basis would they rest their right? They might, indeed, claim or possess the power, but they could not vindicate the right. To deny the right of a person to himself and to the exercise of all his natural powers, is to deny all right and to appeal to force. But this is the right of each man, and so of all equally. The only limitation arises when the activities of one interfere with the rights of another. It is in determining this margin of rights that the problem really consists.

(3) If a man has a right to himself and to the exercise of his powers, he has a right to the product of his powers; for otherwise he would be unable to

realize his primary right. His life cannot be a mere passive existence. To realize his manhood, he must have food, tools, and, in certain climates, clothing and shelter. He does not find these prepared by nature. He has a right to produce them. His right is not identical with the right to a living. It is the right to produce a living. It entitles him to what he produces, but no more. If he take another man's food, under the pretext that "society owes him a living," he makes three false assumptions: First, that any one owes him a living; second, that society owes this debt, and third, that this man, whose food he takes, is the representative of the society that owes him. The right to produce a living is not a debt at all. Society cannot be held to its payment. Worst of all, another's right to the product of his powers is invaded, if the food be taken. The duty of each man is to respect the right of every other man. The duty of society is to protect each man in this right. The question of a right to a living is one dependent upon several circumstances. If there is food available for ten, and twenty set up this claim, a difficulty will arise. Supposing each of the twenty to have an equal claim, each can have but half what he needs. All may starve and no one can maintain his right to a living. For a man to take his living by force would be to rob the rest and add an injustice to a misfortune. But if ten have produced the food for ten, and ten others press the claim of equal division, what becomes of the rights of the ten who have produced their living? The claim of the idle ten is without foundation. They have no right to the food of the others. Even charity will be difficult in the case imagined, but sharing would be charity.

(4) The question of rights is apparently complicated by the statement that all wealth, as it exists in society, is a social and not an individual product. Take a loaf of bread, for example. This, it is said, represents a host of producers. Not only the baker and the miller and the farmer, but the agricultural implement maker, the wood-chopper who cut the timber in the reaper, the iron-workers who fashioned the iron, the miners, the coal-diggers, the teamsters, the wagon-makers, the horseshoers, the harness-makers, and a vast cloud of other contributors whom we seldom think about, are all co-producers of that identical loaf of bread ; that is, it would not be such as it is if these agencies had not conspired to bring together the conditions of its production. They all have a share in it. By implication, if any one of them were hungry, he might help himself. But which one might ? We have here not only the confusion of rights, but the practical obliteration of them. Is there no one who, above all others, and in opposition to all others, has a right to use this bread ? The workman on whose table it lies paid the baker for it, the baker paid the miller, and the miller paid the farmer for the wheat there is in it. Presumably every co-producer has already received his share for his efforts in producing it. If not, and all want it, it is rather late in the day for the adjudication of claims, and the probability is there will be a free

fight over it. But the question of right is not the question of division. It is prior to the question of division. It must be settled as the basis of any settlement of the question of division on the principle of right. To fight for the bread is to ignore all questions of right. To ask for the equities is to assume that there is a moral law of division. When the division of claims has been made in accordance with its law, and each claim has been met, what becomes of the social property in the bread? It is a mere mystification. The bread belongs wholly and absolutely to the man who has bought it and paid for it. He has discharged all claims upon it. Neither society nor any other man than its owner has a right to a crumb of it.

(5) The mist now descends upon the question of rights from still another source. The loaf belongs to the man who has earned it by his labor, but has not society a claim upon it through its claim upon him? Society has made him what he is. It has protected him, it has educated him, it has furnished him a chance to labor. Is there not here a social limitation of individual rights? Yes, without question, the man is indebted for many services rendered. For these he ought to pay. The cost of them, so far as it can be ascertained, ought to be made out, and then with all the rest, sharing like advantages, he should pay his proportion of the cost. This is the justification of taxation. If he enjoys a state of society where public roads are used and public schools have shed light along the path, he certainly

ought to pay for all this. But when this is done can he eat his loaf without a mortgage upon it? No, we are told, he must still share it with the poor and unfortunate. But he insists that he has done that in paying his taxes, and has already remembered the poor. When at last can he hope to sit down to an undivided loaf? Who are these poor that are still unprovided for? What is their claim? It is simply the cry of the poor who are always with us, pleading for charity, not pressing a right. It cannot be formulated as a right without an abuse of language. It is an opportunity for works of mercy, which every Christian man will embrace in his own way, but to call it a "right," to press it as a social obligation that binds a man to action, is to destroy the very possibility of charity in the name of justice.

(6) We conclude, then, that the laborer is at last owner of his bread and has a right to it which cannot be rationally disputed. It is in a peculiar sense "property." That it is private is involved in its very nature. It is the fruit of individual powers, put forth under the protection of rights. It is simply the extension of personality. The right of property is not based upon the possession of it, or upon universal consent. The right may exist where the possession does not, and where consent is not universal. The right precedes all property. It is inherent in man as a personal being. Deny his personality, link him with the lower animals, regard him as a product of nature, the highest note in the music of evolution, and there is no right of property; but then there is

no right whatever. There remains nothing but conflicting forces, the triumph of might and the slavery of the laborer. If the laborer has any rights which he can defend by other means than dynamite, if he has any standing before the tribunal of reason, it is because he is a person, because he is that which Christ taught that he is, the image of God, clothed with the majesty of freedom. Christianity solves this problem of the laborer's rights in the light of its conception of man, the conception that has enfranchised the slave, emancipated woman, and snatched the abandoned child from the eagles and the wolves, to place it in the safety of the cradle and the sunlight of the school.

(7) The right of private property is challenged by some who admit its general principle, when that property assumes the form of land. Henry George insists that the landlord is a monopolist and that all land is in equity the property of society; or, as he puts it, "common property." He does not say, however, to whom it belongs, nor is that possible upon his theory. It belongs to all who are, have been, or ever will be on the earth, and equally. Still, he proposes to tax all the land in the United States to the full extent of the annual rental, and put the money into the United States treasury. There can be little doubt that, if it ever reached that destination, it would be distributed, but it is doubtful if the "ring" would include all the alleged rightful claimants past, present, and to come. It would happen, however, that thousands of honest and industrious laborers,

who have put their lives into the improvement of lands, to say nothing of thousands of helpless widows and orphans whom the departed have left behind, would be rendered homeless and reduced to penury, while the scant three per cent. income which American acres are paying, when other investments are worth twice that percentage, would go into the hands of officials whose places might be more coveted than the mayoralty of New York City. But if we can readily dismiss this preposterous proposition of one who, like other political agitators, lives on the sensation he creates rather than on the labor he glorifies, we may have more respect for John Stuart Mill, when he says: "When the 'sacredness' of property is talked of, it should always be remembered that any such sacredness does not belong in the same degree to landed property. It is the original inheritance of the whole species."[5] The idea of a right of property residing in a "species" is more astonishing than it is intelligible. As the species is indefinite, no individual claim can be determined. How, then, can it be decided whether an individual owner has more or less than his share? If it is to be settled upon the basis of living claimants, even then it would be practically as indefinite. We must first ascertain the amount of land and the number of persons. A plague in Asia or the submergence of an island in Polynesia would seriously disturb boundaries. If the earth belongs to the "species," the rent of this continent does not belong to the United States

[5] Mill's Principles of Political Economy, book ii, chap. i.

treasury, and when collected a portion should be sent to Belgium, where the population is exceedingly crowded, and, indeed, disbursed throughout the globe, in the form of Christmas presents, based on the territorial distribution. In that case, it would pay to keep away from the land altogether and the taxes would be reduced and dividends increased by going to sea. Herbert Spencer goes to the root of the question, as a question of theory, and it is simply that, rather than one for practice. He says: "Equity does not permit property in land. For if one portion of the earth's surface may justly become the possession of an individual and may be held by him for his sole use and benefit as a thing to which he has an exclusive right, then other portions of the earth's surface may be so held; and eventually the whole of the earth's surface; and our planet may thus lapse altogether into private hands."[6] I do not pause to show that no land is held over which society does not enjoy eminent domain and the right of way for compensation, or that too extensive landholding is practically unprofitable, or that land is regarded as common property in certain parts of the world without perceptible advantage, or that, as Laveleye has shown, land was originally held as tribal property, and private property is the only *régime* under which improvement has taken place; but adhere to the purely theoretical and imaginary form in which the argument is stated. Herbert Spencer defends private property in commodities and

[6] Spencer's Social Statics, part ii, chap. ix.

copyrights. Not being a landowner, but deriving his income from royalties on his books, he sees a great injustice in private ownership of the soil, but none in taxing the people for truth, or such approximations to it as he may personally evolve. Let us now, in the same fanciful manner, draw a parallel to Spencer's argument against landowning. "Equity does not permit a man to own the dinner on his table. For, if a man may own one dinner, he may own another, and if two dinners, then ten, and so on, until he might own all the food-supply in the world, and our planet would be reduced to starvation." If this seems very absurd, Spencer's fancy is not less so. There is as much motive for owning all the food as for owning all the land; and more, for less money buys a grain crop than buys a farm, and the power over others would be much greater if one could command all the food than if he owned all the land. As a matter of fact, the food-supply, the coal-supply, and the oil-supply in the United States are more nearly in the control of a few men than the land. There are men in Chicago who know that the grain market can be controlled without owning the land. But if a man cannot own food, he cannot own himself. The argument against the ownership of land lies with equal weight against the owning of one's dinner; but if one cannot own his dinner, he cannot own his body, and if not his body then not his brain, and if not his brain, then not the products of it; hence Herbert Spencer has no equitable property in his copyright!

(8) We conclude that the laborer has the right to the fruit of his labor, and the whole fruit of it, after he has satisfied the like rights of others. This is his right, if there be any ethical foundation of society or any moral nature in man. But there is another aspect of this problem of the rights of the laborer. All that he is and all the natural agents which he employs are bestowments of a higher Power. While no man may interfere with his use of his powers and the fruits of his toil expended upon the materials and forces of nature, there is a claim that underlies all — the claim of the Creator. Christ has presented this neglected aspect of the problem in his parable of the talents. Behind this fortification of rights in which the producer of wealth intrenches himself and protects himself from all invasion of rights, is that citadel of duty which gives security to them all. It is into this that the defender of his rights must at last retire when pressed by his enemies. He says: "I have duties to perform to my family, to my friends. If you take away my rights, I cannot perform my duties. I am bound to realize manhood, and my rights must be accorded that I may perform my duties." This is the Christian solution of the origin of rights. It says to the laborer: This is your land, for you have cleared its swamps and blasted out its rocks and made it golden with a harvest; this is your grain, for you have dropped the dry seeds into the moist earth at springtime and have harvested and winnowed and garnered it; this is your gold, for you have burrowed into the moun-

tains for it and washed away the sand from it until it glitters in your hand; but remember, there is upon it all a claim that you must recognize — the claim of Him who fashioned the mountains and hollowed out the valleys and buried the bright nuggets deep in the rocks for you to gather; the claim of a Father who has placed you among brethren who are like yourself, equal in moral dignity to yourself, if not in powers or possessions, to whom also he has given rights, and whose burdened backs and wearied hands you cannot, as a man and a brother, cause to toil and ache to heap up your treasures or feed your pride. Christianity, respecting and defending every right of man because he is man, with one hand holds the shield of a protecting goddess over the rights of property, and with the other uplifts the sword of justice against the robber and the oppressor. The right of property is simply the right of a steward to discharge his trust without interference. But "it is required in stewards that a man be found faithful."

The increase of wealth is attended with great perils, yet Christianity favors and aids that increase. All the sages and philosophers of antiquity dreaded the day when the simplicity of poverty should give place to the luxury of wealth. They had good reason for this fear, for no pagan nation has ever grown rich without the deterioration of its people. A prophetic psalm of ancient Israel expresses a wish which no pagan sage had dared to utter, but only in view of a condition that renders riches safe. " God be merciful unto us, and bless us, and cause his face to shine upon us, that thy ways may be known upon the earth, thy saving health among all nations. . . . *Then* shall the earth yield her increase; and God, even our own God, shall bless us."

IV.

CHRISTIANITY AND THE PROBLEMS OF WEALTH.

CHRISTIANITY AND THE PROBLEMS OF WEALTH.

I. THE PROBLEM OF DISTRIBUTION.
  1. The Problem an Old One.
  2. Its Contemporary Complications.
  3. The Discussion of the Problem.
  4. Christ's Refusal to be a Divider.
  5. Christianity gives the Spirit, but not the Science of a Solution.
  6. The Method of Arbitration.

II. SCHEMES FOR EQUALIZING WEALTH.
  1. The Postulate of Socialism.
  2. The History and Literature of Socialism.
  3. The Equality of Men a False Assumption.
  4. The Injustice of Equalizing Wealth.
  5. The Fruits of Labor determined by Social Utility.
  6. The Specific Forms of Socialism:
      (1) Revolutionary Socialism;
      (2) Agrarian Socialism;
      (3) State Socialism;
      (4) Christian Socialism.
  7. Did Christ teach Human Equality?

III. THE EQUITABLE DISTRIBUTION OF WEALTH.
  1. Progressive Acquisition.
  2. Decentralizing Agencies.
  3. The Case of the Proletarian.
  4. Industrial Partnerships.
  5. Labor Organizations.
  6. The World as a School of Morals.
  7. Christian Beneficence.

IV.

CHRISTIANITY AND THE PROBLEMS OF WEALTH.

I.

1. When wealth has been produced, there arises the problem of its distribution. It is not a new problem, as the history of the conflicts of capital and labor reveals. Ever since the banquet board of life has been spread for men, they have been crowding one another for the best places. But the conditions are ever changing. In earlier times, large classes gave up all hope of a place at the table, and were content to eat a few crumbs in a corner. It is not so to-day. The results of the republican movement of thought are felt throughout the civilized world. Men everywhere feel that they are as good as others; and, as a Hibernian once said, sometimes a great deal better! Political equality has become so general that social elevation is the dream of the lowest. But it is by no means the intention of any to surrender their places. The same strong desire for personal superiority, as distinguished from personal excellence, that has always been so powerful a motive in men, is still active, and never more so than in our own land and time. In truth, the motive for elevation is even more predominant than ever. The cause

of this lies in the almost universal presumption of the least fortunate people that all misfortune can be effaced by the possession of wealth. The rush for the banquet is never so prompt and energetic as when the crowd is hungry, and the politically enfranchised bring a good appetite to the scene of wealth's distribution.

2. While the problem is thus made a pressing one, there are several circumstances that tend to render it complex. One is the unprecedented division of labor, so minute that almost every commodity is a social product. When a barbarian carved a stone into a hatchet with his own hands, there could be no doubt to whom it belonged; but when a schoolboy purchases a penknife, an army of co-producers rises behind it, each, it may be, with some unsatisfied claim upon it. Another source of difficulty is found in the vast but incalculable progress in the use of mechanical implements and forces, which renders it troublesome to ascertain how large a share of the world's general advancement may fall to each member of society. For example: There is no patent on the use of steam. It has become a human inheritance to which no class has an exclusive right. What proportion of this common advantage should each person enjoy? It is said that, although there has been marvelous progress in the production of wealth, there are classes, and these the hardest worked of all, who have not received a perceptible increment of benefit from this and other heirlooms of humanity. The rhetorical author of " Progress

and Poverty" does not deny the absolute improvement of workingmen in civilized countries, but he formulates this alleged though not clearly proved disproportion of benefit in the telling but false aphorism, "The rich are growing richer, and the poor, poorer."[1] It does not mollify the aroused sense of indignation at this apparent injustice, to be told that many of the greatest fortunes have been acquired by men who began life as wage-earners, and that some of the most gigantic estates in the world have been amassed in one or two generations. This is, in fact, the greatest provocation to the envious, that a man in a nominally free country should rise so rapidly above his fellows as in a few short years to "bestride the narrow world like a colossus."

3. The general diffusion of intelligence and the accessibility of information on every subject have conspired to convert the more advanced countries into a vast indignation meeting, where the most vigorous debate on the constitution of society and the schemes for its reconstruction that has ever resounded in the "parliament of man" is at present rolling its tide of spasmodic eloquence and untrained logic upon the understanding and the conscience of this generation. The political economist has heard the definitions and pretended axioms of his "dismal science" mutilated and denounced, ridiculed and

---

[1] For a statistical refutation of Henry George's statement, "The rich are growing richer, and the poor, poorer," see Rae's Contemporary Socialism, chap. ix; and Mallock's Property and Progress, essay on The Statistics of Agitation.

refuted, and dismissed as impotent to govern thought or dictate action. The socialistic theorist has proposed the most radical and revolutionary remedies, and his more excited cohorts of agitators have disturbed the discussion with bomb and pistol, till it has been found necessary to eject them from the world as conspiring assassins. The Christian minister has preached the precepts of peace with various degrees of comprehension of the debate, and with alternating sympathies with his friends among the rich and among the poor, generally with the result of producing the impression that his sentiments were good and his intentions commendable, but sometimes with a sneer that his salary was paid by the men who could spare the money, and with the intimation that it is not "peace" but "justice" that men want.

4. If we seriously ask, Has Christianity any relation to the problem of wealth's distribution? we shall at once recall the words of Christ, when the young man came to him, saying, "Master, speak to my brother, that he divide the inheritance with me." And Jesus answered: "Man, who made me a judge or a divider over you?" Then follows that pregnant passage which no theory of the distribution of wealth can afford to ignore. Turning to the multitude, he said: "Take heed, and beware of covetousness; for a man's life consisteth not in the abundance of the things which he possesseth. And he spake a parable unto them, saying, The ground of a certain rich man brought forth plentifully; and he thought within himself, saying, What shall I do, because I have no

room where to bestow my fruits? And he said, This will I do: I will pull down my barns, and build greater; and there will I bestow all my fruits and my goods. And I will say to my soul, Soul, thou hast much goods laid up for many years; take thine ease, eat, drink, and be merry. But God said unto him, Thou fool! this night thy soul shall be required of thee; then whose shall those things be which thou has provided? So is he that layeth up treasure for himself, and is not rich toward God." What ground have we for thinking that if Christ were in the flesh to-day he would give another answer? What authority has any disciple of his, in his name, to give another? The plain duty of Christians is to understand and apply this teaching. It involves: (1) a rebuke to covetousness; (2) the declaration that true wealth does not consist in earthly possessions; (3) the necessity of riches toward God, or spiritual attainment.

5. Has Christianity, then, no relation to this subject? May not Christian men attempt the problem of distribution? Certainly we are not assuming to be dividers over men when we seek to ascertain the principles of right division. We are producers of wealth, we have a share in it, and we must know how to divide it among ourselves. If we may draw any practical lesson from Christ's unwillingness to act as judge, it is that he had no principle to apply that men might not by themselves discover. He has elsewhere recommended that differences be settled by agreement and, if that is impossible, by calling in an

arbitrator. He chose not to arbitrate in this case for reasons that are not, indeed, expressed, but are certainly implied. He referred at once to "covetousness." The brother who had the inheritance doubtless had it in accordance with the law. The claimer may have been disinherited for his vices, may have possessed and wasted his share of the fortune, may have been utterly incapable, intellectually and morally, of its proper management. Christ states the spirit with which wealth ought to be regarded. That is really what men need. Victor Hugo once said: "Social philosophy is, in essence, science and peace." Christianity commands that we approach this question in "peace," but our own faculties may discover the "science."

6. Arbitration is rightly represented as the Christian method of settling disputes over wealth. It possesses the advantage of pursuing the way of peace. But it lacks science. With the best of intentions, men may miss the mark of justice if they do not know on what principles to proceed. If there were an omnipresent paternal umpire, endowed with perfect wisdom and impartiality, to administer justice in every case, arbitration would realize perfect equity. But when we consider how complicated are the phenomena, how unwilling men are to expose their affairs to other persons, and how reluctant the disappointed one is likely to be in accepting a decision, and add to all this the innumerable cases in which the tedious process has to be applied, it is evident that it is not as easy as it is sometimes represented

to be. Available in the larger interests of international disputes, because of the comparative infrequency of the occasions when it must be invoked, it is less powerful in the presence of the personal distribution of property. And yet, it is not only the best means we have, but has proved exceedingly useful in France and England, where it has been for years the favorite method of deciding differences between workmen and their employers. The history of arbitration in trade often reads like a romance, and is a perfect vindication of the wisdom of pacific adjustments. On the dark background of waste and violence occasioned by strikes, it shines out like a fiery cross in the heavens, the symbol of blended sacrifice and justice. But even for peaceful arbitration, we need general principles. Once discovered, they may be recognized by all as furnishing the basis of voluntary agreement; or, if not left to personal choice, they may be incorporated into the law of the land, which is the generalized agreement of a people as to what is right and just.

II.

1. Aristotle, who in many respects has not been surpassed as a political writer, says: "Everywhere inequality is a cause of revolution." He then adds: "Men agree about justice in the abstract, but they differ about proportion; some think that if they are equal in any respect they are equal absolutely; others that if they are unequal in any respect, they

are unequal in all."[2] If he had written to-day, after reading the current doctrines of socialism, the Stagirite could not have expressed himself more wisely. Men believe themselves equal in all but wealth, but feel keenly their inequality in the possession of it. They thence conclude that they ought to be equal in wealth also, and every socialistic theory proceeds upon this assumption. In the undiscriminating mind, political equality involves social equality. Men who are not equal in fact imagine that they are by right. Socialism, however it is judged in the light of its proposals, must at least be credited with an ethical impulse. It is a dream of impossible remedies for imaginary wrongs. It assumes that all wealth is produced by the labor of society, that it is, therefore, the property of society, and that justice can be realized only by dividing equally that which belongs to all. It does not pause to reflect that the units in society have not equally produced wealth, and that the claim of each is proportional to his productive contribution. It perceives in the actual condition of men a separation of wealth from its alleged producers, a partition of products by which capital, the creation of labor, is placed on one side of a line and labor, empty-handed, on the other; while existing law creates an impassable barrier between them, excluding the laborer from the fruits of his labors and obliterating every right by the legalized institution of wrong. It proposes by various means to break through this barrier and to divide this wealth among all men.

[2] Aristotle's Politics, book v, 1.

2. This is socialism in its generic outline. It has, however, assumed chameleon forms and wears as many masks as Proteus himself. Its history has been so often repeated in the numerous popular books called out by the contemporary demand, like those of Woolsey, Rae, Laveleye, and Ely, to mention only a few, that any outline even of its historic development through the writings of its forerunners, the Communists, Babœuf, Cabet, Saint-Simon, Fourier, Louis Blanc, Proudhon, and Owen, and its own doctrinaires, Rodbertus, Karl Marx, Lasalle, and their followers, would be a work of supererogation. All these doctrines have been lately stated, expounded, and criticized by numerous able writers, among them a number of distinguished clergymen, such as Doctors Brown, Behrends, Lorimer, Gladden, Smyth, Newton, and others, who have discussed the bearings of these theories both upon the social order and the ethical life. A brief summary and examination of socialistic doctrines, therefore, in the presence of so much available literature, is all that is to be attempted before we proceed to the wider relations which our plan contemplates.

3. The primary assumption of socialism, often latent rather than expressed, is that men are equal. It is a false assumption. They are not equal in powers, either physical or mental, in skill, or in industry. They are, therefore, unequal in production. Some produce only a bare subsistence, and a few not even this. Others create a considerable surplus. Improgressive labor consumes the whole

of its product, while progressive labor accumulates an excess.[3] The producers of wealth are also unequal in their needs. Science certainly contributes to the creation of wealth, but the man of science cannot live as the day-laborer lives. He must be sustained during a long period of preparation, must be supplied with books and appliances, and must enjoy opportunities of travel. The chemist and the coal-heaver are both laborers, but under unequal conditions of necessary expense and surroundings. Men are unequal also in their achievements, even when they have expended the same amount of energy. More depends upon the judicious direction of power than upon its quantity. It is impossible to measure value by days of labor. One man will do in one day what another will not do so well in two or, possibly, cannot do at all. Such a standard is as absurd as an elastic yardstick. No *a priori* mathematical conception of equality can solve the problem of distribution. The units are unequal and the laws of the equation are, therefore, not applicable. The prime error of socialism consists in importing this mathematical idea of an equation into a province of variable units.

4. If each laborer has a right to the whole fruits of his labor, which we have demonstrated in discussing the problem of the laborer's rights, equal participation in wealth involves the moral paradox of

[3] It may be well for the reader to recur to the distinction between improgressive and progressive labor, as given in Lecture III, p. 69, if this distinction is not clearly understood.

taking from one who has a greater right and bestowing upon one who has a less right. Equality in distribution is, therefore, a repudiation of the ethical idea. It cannot be justified on a basis of right. Equality is not equity, if the units who are to participate are unequal. "From each according to his powers, to each according to his needs," is Louis Blanc's monstrous axiom of distribution. It is but a euphemism for the spoliation of the able and industrious for the benefit of the weak and idle. When rendered compulsory, as socialism proposes, it is a new form of slavery. That it is an inversion of the old slavery which subjected the weaker to the stronger, does not render it more acceptable. It proposes to enslave the few who are strong by the combined action of the weak. The pigmies may shackle the giant, but first they must put out his eyes. Like another Samson, he would at last end his bondage in wreck and ruin. The individual cannot be thus deprived of freedom, but if he were, the servile spirit would inevitably survive when hope was dead, and weakness and idleness would be preferred to strength and industry. The grand motive in the creation of wealth is the expectation of its enjoyment. The adoption of Louis Blanc's aphorism, or any compulsory equivalent, would paralyze labor and introduce an epoch of industrial stagnation and pauperism.

5. The value of a day's labor depends upon its relation to social need. Social utility is the quality in labor that responds to that need and affords it

satisfaction. It may require as much force to produce a thousand coats that will not fit as to produce the same number of well-fitting garments, or to produce them out of season as in the season when they are needed. But there is obviously a great difference with reference to social need. The well-cut garments will all be sold at a good price, while the others must be sold for less, or remain unsold. A man with a pile of clothes too small for him is hardly better off than a man without any. The socialists overlook this element of quality in labor. Karl Marx argues that all capital is produced by labor and then that the laborers are all and equally entitled to share in its possession. But suppose the tailors take for their share the coats they have produced. Some, though they have worked as hard as any, will be rewarded with the ill-fitting garments which are of no use to them, and they are as badly off as if they had received less wages in money than their more skilful fellows. It is evidently unjust to take away from the expert in order to reward the bunglers. It is equally so to rob the successful for the benefit of the unsuccessful. The whole problem of just distribution turns upon the pivot of social utility in response to social need. "Why should the stonebreaker on a railroad receive less money for his time than the engineer of a train, and the engineer less than the president of the company? It is not because it costs more effort to preside over the affairs of the company; it is not because it costs more effort to run the train. So far as the putting forth of measurable energy goes, the order of rewards ought to be reversed, for the stone-breaker puts forth more foot-pounds of force than the other two. It is not a complete answer to say that the cost of preparation is the measure of reward and that the engineer must be paid for the time used in learning to manage the engine, and the president for the time spent in learning to preside over a railroad's affairs. The true answer is this: the service of each man is paid according to its worth to the company. If the stone-breaker will not work, others will take his place for what he receives. If the engineer will not work, others will take his place for what he receives. Wages must always rise to this market-price. But the engineer will not work for what the stone-breaker receives. Why not? Because he can get more for his service. Why can he get more? Because others are willing to pay more. Why are they willing to pay more? Because his service has a higher quality than that of the other man. In what does this quality consist? In elements of knowledge, skill, and judgment, in power to do safely and certainly what the other cannot do safely and certainly. Put the stone-breaker in charge of the engine and there would be a destructive accident. Put the engineer in charge of the president's business and there would be unskilful management of the company's affairs, involving loss and possible bankruptcy. It may be settled as certain that the company would not pay the engineer any more than the stone-breaker, if it could hire him for the same.

Service has social utility in proportion as it rises in the scale of skill and efficiency. The stone-breaker is little more than a machine, so far as his occupation goes. A machine has been invented to take his place. As power advances from the merely physical to the intellectual and moral orders, it becomes more valuable."[4]

6. The specific forms of socialism all share, to some extent, in the generic fallacy of the doctrine. They all propose by artificial means to unite suddenly capital and labor in the same hands.

(1) Revolutionary socialism, as represented by the International Workmen's Association, aims to do this by universal confiscation and redistribution of wealth. The political socialists of this school would accomplish their end by the votes of the people, but this method is usually seen to be impracticable, since it implies as its precondition a mental revolution that argument cannot produce. The anarchic branch of this school proposes the overthrow of the present order by physical force and intimidation. Its only argument is dynamite. This is a phase of the question with which policemen and magistrates alone can deal.

(2) Agrarian socialism sees a solution of the problem in the confiscation and nationalization of land, not by purchase, but by legal compulsion through insufferable taxation. This is the prescription of Henry George for the ills of society. It is needless

[4] Quoted from my brochure on The Principles and Fallacies of Socialism, No. 533 of Lovell's Library.

to dwell upon the injustice of this crude remedy; but, if applied, would it better any one's condition? If the form of change were simply that present holders of land should pay the whole rent for taxes, they would, in subletting, double the rent, which would increase the price of bread, since rent enters into the price of the products of land, so that non-landholders would have both increased rent and increased cost of food, while the money thus raised would go in part to public improvements and in part to government officials. If the change involved the actual expulsion of landholders from their estates, it would provoke a war for the hearthstone that could not be suppressed. This agrarian socialism of George has all the ethical faults of revolutionary socialism with the additional trait of logical absurdity. As another has said: " He would not tax a palace, but the plot under it. He would not tax a line of steamships, but their wharf. He would not tax a lump of gold, but the hole in the ground out of which it was dug." [5]

(3) State socialism is a more subtle but equally inadequate solution. It proposes to solve the problem of distribution by adding two new functions to the State: the *reparative*, undertaking to repair the evils of too great private possessions, by fixing a maximum beyond which one may not own property and by wholly or partly abolishing the right of inheritance; and the *assistive*, awarding grants to workmen for employment, insurance, and industrial enterprise.

[5] Man's Birthright, by E. H. G. Clark, introduction.

This system has numerous adherents in Germany, among them the great chancellor, Prince Bismarck, and many university professors known as "Socialists of the Chair." [6] Some American students of political and social science in Germany have imported some of these neo-economic notions into our own country, and have given them a certain popularity through newspapers, magazines, and reviews. The so-called "historic" method, which characterizes the new school, is excellent in teaching us what to avoid, but easily imparts to the mind a retrogressive tendency. The worst vice of these economic critics, however, is an crudite vagueness which, in attempting to attain to the unknown, renders very nebulous the whole province of the known. They write rhetorically about the ethical element in economic theory, without pointing out with clearness the basis of right, or showing precisely how rights may be realized. Social theories that have no better title to acceptance than flings at the immorality of the classic economists present a very poor *prima facie* case. Mackintosh says: "I have known Adam Smith slightly, Ricardo well, Malthus intimately. Is it not something to say for a science, that its three great masters were about the three best men I ever knew?" [7] It is sometimes forgotten that

[6] Notably Professor Adolph Wagner, of the University of Berlin, who has formulated a "law of increasing extension of the functions of public power" (Grundlegung, p. 308), and would both limit inheritance and enforce state insurance for workingmen.

[7] Quoted by Professor Edwin R. A. Seligman, in Science Economic Discussion, p. 14.

the founder of that much-reproached science which assumes that self-interest is the principal factor in the world of wealth, was also the author of an ethical system founded wholly upon sympathy, and bearing for its motto, "Put yourself in his place." The neologists condemn the wage-system, or system of free personal contract between employer and employed, as utterly unworthy of our civilization. But they offer nothing better. There are vague allusions to the "extension of state action," but no precise methods are pointed out by which the State may control the distribution of wealth, without the invasion of personal rights which we Americans are accustomed to hold dear. It may be modestly questioned if these writers have not imported a temporary phase of German speculation, conceived largely under the influence of a government that desires to ingratiate itself into the affections of the people by the performance of paternal functions, in order to render permanent an empire but newly created.[a] This new doctrine of the

[a] In a speech delivered on the third of January, 1882, Bismarck said: "I have already explained the system which I am come to uphold, according to the instructions of His Majesty the Emperor. We wish to establish a state of things in which no one can say 'I exist only to bear social burdens, and nobody takes thought of my fate.' Our dynasty has for a long time been endeavoring to reach this object. Frederick the Great already describes this mission in saying, 'I am king of the beggars,' and he realized it in administering strict justice. Frederick William III gave freedom to the peasants. Our present sovereign is animated by the noble ambition to put a hand, in his old age, to the work of assuring to the least favored and weakest of our fellow-citizens, if not the same rights that were seventy years ago granted to the peasantry, at least a decided amelioration in their condition, in order that they can count upon the help of the State." "The whole theory of state socialism, and of a socialist monarch, is summed up in this passage," says Laveleye, from whom I quote it. The Socialism of To-day, chap. vi.

growing dominance of the State, and diminution of the individual, will be found as repugnant to American independence as the lofty German theories of transcendentalism, not less ably or enthusiastically urged upon the American mind a generation ago, proved to our Yankee common-sense. For scholarly young gentlemen, whose reputations are yet in the nascent condition, and whose chosen department of study does not afford the brilliant discoveries of physical science, the introduction of novelties seems a natural policy, and "Omne ignotum pro magnifico," an excellent motto; but it will require diligence, if in their remaining years, they convince the American people that it is either sensible or just to say that a man may possess ninety-nine thousand, nine hundred and ninety-nine dollars and ninety-nine cents, but not one hundred thousand dollars; that it is a higher form of justice to give the whole or a part of a child's patrimony to the public than to the child for love of whom its father laboriously earned and prudently saved it; that it is a national good to employ workmen with money from the public treasury in order to give them employment, under the management of public officials whose morals might not be better than those of some customs officers, or to insure men's lives, or to start workmen in coöperative industry. In France, in 1848, Louis Blanc's idea of state subsidies for coöperation among workmen were so far carried into effect that "thirty associations, twenty-seven of which were composed of workmen, . . . received eight hundred and ninety thousand, five hundred francs. Within six months three of the Parisian societies failed ; and of the four hundred and thirty-four associates, seventy-four resigned, fifteen were excluded, and there were eleven changes of managers. In July, 1851, eighteen associations had ceased to exist. One year later twelve others had vanished. In 1865, four were still extant, and had been more or less successful. In 1875, there was but a single one left." [9] Such are the historic lessons of state intervention for the just distribution of wealth. It is more likely to facilitate distribution than to secure justice.

4. It is claimed by the Christian socialists that what the law cannot do in that it is weak, the spirit of Christianity can do in that it is strong. They would equalize wealth by religious beneficence, voluntarily raising and depositing in the hands of workingmen large sums of money for coöperative industry. Forty years ago the communist Villegardelle compiled a volume of extracts from the Christian Fathers, to show that social property is the Christian ideal. Bishop Ketteler, of Mayence, was a friend of Lasalle and wrote a book in 1864 on "The Labor Question and Christianity," depicting modern society as the revolutionary socialists do, acknowledging all the evils of which they complain. Upon this basis he offered an eloquent plea for voluntary contributions from all good Catholics for socialistic experiments. A host of others have followed in his

[9] Laveleye, op. cit. p. 73, note.

train, until there is now in Germany a strong contingent of Catholic socialists, strangely enough united politically with the atheistic socialists to forward the schemes of industrial revolution. Quickened to action by the apparent success of the Catholics in leading the minds of workingmen, and fearful of losing all hold on that class through lack of sympathy with its misfortunes, the evangelical Christians of Germany, headed by Dr. Stöcker, the eloquent court preacher at Berlin, have also organized a socialistic movement.[10] Herr Todt places the following epigraph at the head of his book on "Radical German Socialism and Christianity": "Whoever would understand the social question and contribute to its solution must have on his right hand the works on political economy and on his left the literature of scientific socialism, and must keep the New Testament open before him." "Political economy explains the social anatomy, scientific socialism describes the disease, and the gospel indicates the cure." But the masses who are inclined to socialistic ideas quite generally repudiate the "socialists in surplice" and prefer the "socialists in blouse." The movement has made more converts to socialism among Christians than it has converts to Christianity among socialists. Said Herr Most at a joint meeting at which Dr. Stöcker was present: "The social democracy will not recede; it will pursue its course and accomplish its

---

[10] The views of Dr. Stöcker are set forth in his address on "Die Bibel und die Sociale Frage," delivered before the Evangelical Labor Union at Nürnberg, which has passed through many editions.

designs, even though all priestdom should rise against it, like a cloud of locusts thick enough to darken the sun. The social democracy knows that the days of Christianity are numbered, and that the time is not far distant when we shall say to the priests, Settle your account with heaven, for your hour has come." [11] It is clear that oil and water are not more repugnant to coalescence than are Christianity and socialism, considered as types of thought and feeling. Maurice and Kingsley are well known as advocates of what has been called Christian socialism in England, but their doctrines are wholly different from those of the German socialists.[12] "Competition," said Maurice, "is put forth as a law of the universe. That is a lie. The time has come for us to declare that it is a lie by word and deed. I see no way but associating for work instead of for strikes." "It is my belief," said Kingsley, "that not self-interest, but self-sacrifice, is the only law upon which human society can be grounded with any hope of prosperity and permanence." These are appeals for order and renunciation rather than for revolution and reprisal.

7. But it is now time to ask seriously, Did Christ teach the equality of men or favor the equalization of possessions? When the ambitious mother of Zebedee's children came to him, saying, "Grant

---

[11] Quoted by Laveleye, op. cit. chap. vii.

[12] Some account of Christian Socialism in England is given by Laveleye, op. cit., supplementary chapter; and by Ely, in his French and German Socialism in Modern Times, chap. xiv.

that these my two sons may sit, the one on thy right hand, and the other on the left, in thy kingdom," Jesus replied that she knew not what she asked, and disclosed to her the conditions on which this preëminence depends. "To sit on my right hand and on my left, is not mine to give, but it shall be given to them for whom it is prepared of my Father." Inequality and preëminence are not denied, even in the kingdom of heaven, but preëminence is not an arbitrary gift ; it is prepared for the deserving in the divine order. Jesus goes on to explain that among the nations preëminence is based upon dominion, or lordship, but in the kingdom of heaven, on service. "Whosoever will be great among you, let him be your minister; and whosoever will be chief among you, let him be your servant." Economic greatness is founded upon power, moral greatness is founded upon love. Inequality was recognized in both and not condemned in either. Whatever the opinions of the fathers may be, Christ does not commend equality in the distribution of wealth. If it be asserted that equality is taught in the brotherhood of man, it is sufficient to note that brothers, equal in nature, are not equal in personal powers, personal productiveness, or personal deserts. In the case where Christ was appealed to as judge between brothers, he showed no concern that they be regarded as possessing equal claims, probably because he thought that in equity they were unequal.

III.

1. The equitable division of wealth, which cannot be realized by artificial aids to equality, may nevertheless be attained by other means. I say the "*equitable*" division, not the "equal" division. This proceeds on the assumption that capital should be placed in the hands of labor only by progressive acquisition. It is nature's universal method, the method of growth, illustrated in every province of being, from the formation of a crystal to the consolidation of a character. Suddenly acquired wealth seldom remains long in its possessor's hands, or finds its place there even briefly without demoralizing results. The creation of wealth is in its nature a moral discipline, involving industry, patience, temperance, and self-sacrifice. Wealth, like preëminence in the moral world, offers its reward normally only to those who have been prepared in the divine order to receive it. Without its virtues, it may, indeed, be dishonestly acquired, but it cannot be permanently retained.

2. The mechanism of distribution is much more perfect than we are wont to fancy. The wealth which one generation accumulates, the next scatters. Close observers hold that it is unusual for business success to remain in the same family for more than three generations. Within the same generation the centrifugal forces are acting. We see the successes of men, but they conceal their failures. In 1881, Dun & Co., the well-known commercial agents, re-

ported that fifty per cent. of the wholesale merchants doing business in Chicago in 1870 had failed in that single decade. One well acquainted with such affairs says that not more than three per cent. of those who embark in trade end life with success. But, from the nature of it, wealth can be enjoyed only by being distributed. The owner of a vaultful of gold has no wealth in any true sense, until he unlocks the vault and disburses the gold. He cannot gratify the first desire without contributing to the social need. If he wishes interest, he must place his dollars in the hands of one who needs them and can use them. If he would enjoy a dinner, obtain a carriage, or build a mansion, he must put his coins in the hands of cooks, wheelwrights, or architects, who in turn pass them on to others. There is no wealth that does not respond to social need. My lord the Duke of Westminster, with his millions of acres and scores of palaces, cannot have his dinner to-day, except on condition that the cook and the butler have theirs also.

3. But what shall we say of the man who has no means of satisfying social need? There is no such man, unless he is an idiot, a lunatic, an invalid, or the victim of some misfortune. He then becomes an object of charity, and his case we shall consider later. But the so-called "proletarian" can supply social need. Men are too valuable to be allowed to starve in an industrial age. As Count Tolstoï has said, "Laborers are necessary. And those who profit by labor will always be careful to provide the

means of labor for those who are willing to work."[13] Why should a man who can do nothing for himself complain if he lives upon the lowest plane? If he can do better, let him do so freely. If he is not above the status of the Pilgrim Fathers, let him take up some unimproved land and raise a crop of wheat. If he can, let him learn a trade and rise in it. It is the old way, but it is the only honest, manly way. If, as Hæckel says, the development of the individual man is a summary and epitome of the development of the race, let him begin where Adam did, among the fruit-trees, and work his way up. Away with the sentimentalism and snobbishness of socialism and of semi-socialism, which scoff at the dignity of labor and ridicule the hands of toil. We are not better than our fathers. The proletarian of to-day may be the President of to-morrow, as several of our ablest have been. The true American does not want an equality which he has not earned. He wants to be a man, free to labor where and how he chooses, with liberty of contract and wages proportioned to his usefulness as estimated by his fellows, and through manhood to become the equal of any in the life of freedom and self-conscious nobility.

4. No doubt much may be hoped for from industrial partnership and coöperation. There is not a village in the land where there are not men who have risen from poverty to independence by this method. But no enterprise will succeed where there is not ability to plan and manage. It ought not to succeed

---

[13] Count Tolstoï's My Religion, chap. x.

without it. It would be putting a premium on stupidity and inefficiency. It is such ability that finds large rewards as wages of superintendence. If coöperating laborers can supply this among themselves, or pay for it, they can have it; but if not, they will fail. Whatever may be said in abuse of the wage-system, it shows the superiority of brains to muscle. Voluntary profit-sharing on the part of employers may be judicious, experience must decide this; but profit-sharing cannot be logically disassociated from loss-sharing, which in the end might leave small advantage to employees. The practicability of this system has been ably advocated by Sedley Taylor in his interesting little book on "Profit-sharing," but it implies a noble altruism not attributed to the "economic man." In spite of his enthusiasm as an advocate of this plan, that writer closes his preface with the "profound conviction that the methods described in this volume, valuable as they are in themselves, constitute no panacea; and that their best fruits can be reaped only by men who feel that life does not consist in abundance of material possessions, who regard stewardship as nobler than ownership, who see in the ultimate outcome of all true work issues reaching beyond the limits of the present dispensation, and who act faithfully and strenuously on these beliefs."[14] Enforced profit-sharing, like enforced arbitration, is a pure chimera. It is essentially socialistic, invading the right of contract, and will never be tolerated by a free people. Here, as every-

---

[14] Sedley Taylor's Profit-sharing between Capital and Labor, preface.

where in the discharge of the social functions, Christianity alone can solve the problem. If all men were Christians, the labor problem would melt away and be forgotten in the sense of universal brotherhood. Until they are, there is no cure for the evils born of human greed.

5. The organization of labor may legitimately accomplish much, especially in mutual help and insurance. So far as labor organizations aim at creating fraternal feelings among workingmen, the improvement of the trades, the discovery of needs, and the distribution of men where they are wanted, they are highly commendable and may prove useful. But as human nature is constituted, they threaten to become the most oppressive monopolies in the land, binding the wills and consciences of men, forcing upon them actions contrary to their judgments and their interests; as when, in the strikes among the coal-heavers in New York, men receiving $20 per week, promptly and satisfactorily paid, were forced by their executive committee into the ridiculous position, in order to give moral support, of striking for thirty-three per cent. less than they were receiving! Such centralized corporations, often under the control of petty tyrants who are without reason or conscience, veritable dictators without responsibilities, constitute an *imperium in imperio*, whose power and passion may well be dreaded.

6. The Christian conception of man and the world does not afford any specific criterion for the division of wealth. Man is endowed with moral freedom and

the world is a scene of moral discipline. It is an order in which hope and fear, gain and loss, success and failure, must ever be possible, for they are essential to its purpose. Christ's prayer for his disciples was not that they might be taken out of the world, or that the world might be transformed to give them peace or comfort, but that they might be kept from the evil. It is not what we have, but what we are, that makes life sweet and blessed. Wealth is not simply to gratify but to unfold our natures. Its ministry of sensations passes away, but its ministry of discipline is everlasting. "The true secret of happiness," says Canon Westcott, "is not to escape toil and affliction, but to meet them with the faith that through them the destiny of man is fulfilled, that through them we can even now reflect the image of our Lord and be transformed into his likeness."

7. "The poor," said Jesus, "always ye have with you." I cannot see that it will ever be otherwise. It is proof that Christ entertained no dream of social equality. If all were equalized to-day, there would be the poor, if not the rich, to-morrow. The virtue of beneficence will never be outgrown upon the earth. The incapable, the unfortunate, the sick, to say nothing of the idle and the improvident, will ever sit by the wayside, waiting for the coming of the Good Samaritan. For the Christian, the problem of wealth's distribution is largely one of judicious beneficence, for the world has learned that there is beneficence that is injudicious and even injurious. An undiscriminating charity has fostered mendicancy

and pauperism and there are countries of Europe where no church is without its waiting beggar. William Law, the author of the "Serious Call," gave a literal interpretation to the words of Christ, "Give to him that asketh thee," and with two rich friends resolved to deny himself as much as possible and supply the needs of every applicant. They attracted a great crowd of idle and lying mendicants to the neighborhood, till finally the community had to petition the magistrates to interfere, in order to prevent the utter demoralization of the parish. But suppose we should interpret with similar literalness the saying, "If any man come to me and hate not his father, and mother, and wife, and children, and brethren, and sisters, yea, and his own life also, he cannot be my disciple!" A slow beast needs sharp goads, and Christ stirs and startles the conscience by such awakening words, not as giving laws of action but spurs to reflection. Some counselors, like Herbert Spencer, advise us to follow our own self-interest, without concern for others, with the assurance that all will thus be happier, because more independent. Between the misdirected almsgiving of the purely sympathetic and the indifference of the selfish, lies the narrow way of wisdom, walking in which, Christ says, "Whenever ye will ye may do them good." We are sometimes told that we ought never to give directly, but only through organizations. This counsel overlooks the blessing of personal ministration. The Good Samaritan took a personal pleasure in relieving misfortune. We need the contact with suffering and the lessons of patience and faith which it often teaches. Besides, it is sometimes the gift of ourselves, rather than of our money, it is our counsel, our sympathy, our word of cheer, that would make glad the heart and infuse strength. I have no word of criticism for the noble work of organized charity, but there is much that it cannot do, because it lacks the human personality which in God's order, both for the recipient and the bestower, should be present in every ministration. And, as a rule, the best gift is the one that has most of personality in it. All true strength radiates outward from the centre. A weak heart or a weak mind needs a strong one. Encouragement, advice, knowledge, a place to work in, a nobler work to do, are better gifts than food and clothing ; for they produce these and confer the power that continues to produce them. The best form of beneficence that the world has discovered is helping others to help themselves.

V.

CHRISTIANITY AND THE PROBLEMS OF MARRIAGE.

CHRISTIANITY AND THE PROBLEMS OF MARRIAGE.

I. THE PROBLEM OF POPULATION.
   1. Immigration from the Cradle.
   2. The Doctrine of Malthus.
   3. The Results of Malthusianism.
   4. The Inadequacy of Malthusianism.

II. THE HISTORY OF THE FAMILY.
   1. The Four Stages of Domestic Evolution.
   2. Monogamy, an alleged Transition.
   3. Socialism and the Family.
   4. Criticism of the Evolution Theory.

III. THE CHRISTIAN CONCEPTION OF THE FAMILY.
   1. Christ's Doctrine of Monogamy.
   2. The Divine Plan in the Family.
   3. The Family as part of the Moral Order.
   4. The Consistency of New Testament Teaching.

IV. THE DOMESTIC STATUS.
   1. The Status of the Child.
   2. The Status of the Wife.
   3. The "Emancipation" of Woman.
   4. The Dissolution of Marriage.

V.

CHRISTIANITY AND THE PROBLEMS OF MARRIAGE.

I.

1. "We occupy an island," says Laveleye, in his work on "Primitive Property," "where we live on the fruits of our labor; a shipwrecked man is thrown up by the sea: What is his right? Can he say, invoking the unanimous opinion of jurisconsults: You have occupied the land by virtue of your title as human beings, because property is the condition of liberty and culture, a necessity of existence, a natural right; but I also am a man, I also have a natural right to make a living; I can, then, occupy with the same title with yourselves a corner of this ground, in order to live here by my labor?"[1] This parable is illustrated whenever a human child arrives in the world, with the addition that the child not only will presently want his corner of the earth in which to make a living, but immediately needs to be cared for and then to be reared to maturity before he can begin his self-support by labor. Shall we give him a place, or shall we push him back into the sea? Humanity says that he must be snatched from the waves, even at the cost of toil and risk of life. But

[1] Laveleye, De la Propriéte et de ses Formes Primitives, p. 393.

here is another mouth to feed and a new subdivision of wealth is inevitable. Evidently, we have before us a social fact that gives rise to important problems. Society has an interest in the growth of population, and, therefore, in the conditions and forms of marriage.

2. The relation of population to subsistence is regarded by Malthus as the central point of all social problems.[2] In this opinion most of the orthodox economists of England substantially concur. The doctrine of Malthus is, that population tends to increase in a geometrical ratio, while the food-supply tends to increase in an arithmetical ratio. In plainer terms, while in four generations of men population tends to repeat itself sixteen times, the food-supply tends to repeat itself only four times. The critics who have attempted to answer Malthus's great and epoch-making "Essay on the Principle of Population" have often done that worthy clergyman the grossest injustice, condemning his doctrine as essentially "immoral" and "infamous," without apprehending his pure and philanthropic motives; and pronouncing his principle "false," without even understanding it. Malthus nowhere says that population and food-supply do actually increase and vary in these ratios, but that they tend to do so. All evidence that they do not so vary which ignores the tendency, and appeals only to the actual state of the case, simply misses the mark. His book is largely occupied in showing why they do not thus vary in

[2] Malthus's Essay on the Principle of Population.

reality, and the reasons are the presence in human history of war, pestilence, and other depopulating causes. These, it is to be hoped, will in time be abolished. What, then, is to prevent the tendency from realizing itself in fact, by a growth of population out of proportion to the growth of food-supply? Malthus answers: "Preventive checks, such as abstention from marriage and temperance in marriage." His remedy for poverty is "prudential restraint" in augmenting the race. If there are not too many mouths to feed, there will be bread enough for all. Such a doctrine is not to be silenced with abuse, for it is evidently based on laws of nature and principles of logic.

3. The Malthusian remedy for poverty and distress is, then, the limitation of marriages, first by public opinion and then by law. Let us examine the foundations upon which the theory rests as an exposition of the cause and cure of poverty. Overpopulation, if it existed anywhere, would certainly cause poverty. There are, no doubt, countries that are too populous for the general good; that they are, is evident from the relief that follows emigration; and yet, no doubt, even more relief might result from better forms of land-tenure and industrial life. The objection offered to Malthusianism by Henry George,[3] that the greater the number of producers the greater will be the wealth produced, does not meet the case; for it disregards the law of diminishing returns in the cultivation of the soil, which must somewhere be

[3] George's Progress and Poverty, chap. iv.

reached by the growth of population. That it has been nowhere reached is irrelevant to the question. It is absurd to say that there cannot be too many people to the acre. Nor does the answer of Herbert Spencer,[4] that such pressure of population would result in the elimination of the weak and feeble, and thus improve the race, constitute an answer to Malthus. Even though this struggle for existence should result in the survival of the fittest, there is no assurance that all might not be deteriorated by the hardships of the competition, as all are in Tierra del Fuego. The just and true criticism upon Malthusianism relates both to its assumptions and its remedies. That theory assumes that the reproductive power will continue to act in geometrical ratio; whereas we know that as organisms rise in the scale of existence reproductive energy is lost. Irish peasants have large families; but the aristocratic families, with abundance, frequently become extinct. It assumes also that the food-supply is capable only of arithmetical increase, whereas scientific agriculture is continually refuting this supposition. Men are better fed to-day, in all civilized lands, than they were when Malthus wrote, notwithstanding the vast increase in numbers. In truth, it requires a dense population to develop natural resources and a nation's wealth consists in its men not less than in its territory. With regard to remedies, Malthusianism, in attempting to cure one evil, creates a worse. In France, where the doctrine of "prudential restraint"

[4] Spencer's Principles of Biology, vol. ii, part vi, chap. xiii.

has been most widely accepted, we see statesmen and physiologists and moralists alike deploring the consequences, while in Paris marriages have decreased, the institution of vice is legally established, and one third of the children are born outside of the bonds of wedlock.[5] Even in Bavaria, where marriage is legally made difficult, there is an exceedingly large percentage of illegitimates.[6] If vice is worse than poverty, Malthusianism is not its best remedy. Nature has secured the perpetuation of the species by instincts too powerful to be annihilated or effectually restrained by legislation, or even entirely by the individual will. If children are not born in the shelter of the home and under the care of responsible parents, they will be thrown into life without other protection than society is prepared to provide, either by law or charity.

4. The fear of poverty is not the most potent restraint upon the practices of men. The proletarian indulges the hope that some of his children may prosper and be of service to him in his declining years. His very name signifies his proclivity. Upon him, therefore, the Malthusian doctrine has but little influence. A stronger motive to abstinence from marriage is found in that pessimism that regards life as a scene of suffering and its end an escape from misery. Buddha was its great apostle in the East, and though his millions of disciples professed to

---

[5] The whole subject is discussed, with valuable recent statistics, by Dr. Abel Joire, La Population, Paris, 1885.

[6] W. Graham's The Social Problem, chap. iii.

believe that life is an evil, and marriage, which is its foundation, is a source of sorrow, the swarming populations of Buddhist countries testify to the impotency of this religious hostility to life in crushing out the instinct to render it perpetual. The country of Schopenhauer and Von Hartmann is the most prolific in Europe, in spite of the pessimism which their philosophy inculcates. The same pessimism that censures marriage commends suicide, and the prohibition of the first is about as rational and effective as the recommendation of the other.

II.

It is certain that no Malthusian precept or pessimistic philosophy will ever prevent the fulfillment of the command to "multiply and replenish the earth." Society cannot, if it would, restrain this tendency; but it has no higher interest, either from an ethical or an economical point of view, than the mode in which this command is obeyed. The germ of society itself is in the family. What is its history and what is its normal constitution?

1. It is apparent upon a little reflection that the same close connection which Malthus points out between population and subsistence, between family life and economic life, must always have existed. A condition of society is inconceivable in which the multiplication of human beings and their support should have no connection. If private property and private marital rights are associated, so are communal property and community of wives. If the study of

primitive peoples reveals communal property, it also reveals a corresponding type of the family. Anthropologists of the evolutionist school, such as Bachofen, McLennan, Spencer, Lubbock, and Giraud-Teulon attempt to trace the evolution of the family from a primitive form in which sexual unions were temporary and promiscuous, as they are in the lower animals.[7] Without adducing their arguments, or for the present criticizing their results, I simply summarize their theory. They recognize four stages of progression: (1) Promiscuity, in which state men and women associate in herds, like other gregarious animals; (2) Polyandry, the union of one woman with many men, whose children trace their descent from their mother and are supported by the group, constituting the "maternal family;" (3) Polygyny, the union of one man with several women, who are under his perpetual authority, and whose children take his name, constituting the "paternal family;" and finally, (4) Monogamy, the union of one man and one woman for life.[8]

2. Consistent evolutionists maintain that the present legalized form of the family is only a transition to some other and unknown type. Says Dr. Letourneau, a French materialistic evolutionist:

---

[7] The latest and most compendious treatment of the whole subject, from the evolutionist's point of view, is that of Giraud-Teulon, Les Origines du Mariage et de la Famille. The Family, an Historical and Social Study, by C. F. and Carrie Butler Thwing, has been published since these lectures were written, and confirms many of the positions taken in them.

[8] For a statement of this order of development as a necessary and established order, see Louis Bridel, La Femme et le Droit.

"In our European marriage, where the barbarous and feudal customs, the legal traditions of ancient Rome and Christian ideas, have arrived at a crippled compromise, woman is neither slave nor servant; she is simply a minor, and the law makes of the conjugal union an association which death alone can dissolve, at least in the majority of Catholic countries. Will it always be so? Evidently not. In the evolution of societies there is no last word. Already, legal divorce, admitted, or upon the point of being admitted, in different countries of Europe, has destroyed the fiction of monogamic and indissoluble marriage. . . . No form of marriage is absolutely necessary, and many forms have been tried. There will, assuredly, still be innovations. In what sense? We can hardly conjecture; but it will surely be in the sense most useful to society. Utility varies with the constitution of societies. Where the State does not interest itself in the rearing of children, a more rigorous monogamy is necessary; the family ought to be solidly constituted, for it will be only in its bosom that new generations can find shelter, protection, education. On the contrary, where individual interests go on uniting themselves more and more, the State will gradually tend to substitute itself for the family in the care of rearing its future citizens. Little by little the State will occupy itself less with the regulation of marriage, and more with the formation of new generations; the care of infancy will become for it a capital interest; sexual unions in themselves will tend to be more and more considered as acts of private life. To raise the child, this is what the community will aspire to accomplish, and it will charge itself more and more with this important care; then it will have no reason for not leaving a much greater latitude to conjugal contracts."[9] Then follows a mocking paragraph on the "sanctuary of the family," which, for very shame, I forbear from quoting.

3. It is impossible to separate the socialistic doctrine of property from the socialistic doctrine of the family. The one places all property in the hands of the State; the other, consistently and even with logical necessity, places the care of children in the same hands where the means of subsistence have been deposited, leaving individuals to become parents under the impulse of elective affinities and the State to rear and educate their offspring! Such has been the teaching of communism and socialism from Plato down to the present. Community of property involves a practical community of wives. Every argument that sustains the former sustains the latter also. I need not overburden this outline with citations to prove the close association between the attacks on private property and the war upon the family. Robert Owen denounced marriage as one of the three curses of society, private wealth and religion being the other two. Fourier commended the abolition of marriage. The socialistic programmes openly proclaim the dissolution of the family as an end to be desired. "Love ought to

---

[9] Letourneau, La Sociologie d'après l'Ethnographie, libre iv, chap. i, xvi.

be free, and relieved from all codes and rituals," says the Havre Programme, which also advocates the support of children at public cost. At an assembly of German socialists in Berlin, one of the orators, Jorissen, said that, in the state of the future, only love should direct the unions of the sexes. Between the wife and the prostitute there was only a quantitative difference, for both sold themselves for a living. Children should belong to the State and be maintained by it.[10] Though not universally accepted by those present, these views were not opposed on any principle and, indeed, could not be by socialists without defect of logic. An American advocate of socialism, Gronlund, regards marriage as merely a "commercial institution," and admits that the new organization of society will "considerably modify marriage," and will "facilitate divorces."[11] It is evident that socialism stands committed to the abolition of the family. The monogamic family is the source of the most potent motive to the acquisition of private wealth. Evidence would be superfluous to show that men who are improvident before marriage become economical and prudent in the family relation. This holds good, notwithstanding the powerful motive to saving in anticipation of marriage. The most efficient protection of private property is that conjugal and parental love that is produced only where two beings are indissolubly united, and paternity is guarded by a strict fidelity.

[10] Woolsey's Communism and Socialism, p. 257.
[11] Gronlund's The Coöperative Commonwealth, chap. x.

It is also the most powerful incentive to personal industry, the mainspring of all wealth creation. Socialistic theorists do not perceive, what is very obvious upon reflection, that a social condition in which women were common, and in which all children were supported by the public, would be one in which idleness and sensuality would drive out industry and affection, the true factors of wealth, and plunge society into universal poverty. Those primitive types of society in which tribal property and tribal marriage were united, were low in the scale of wealth and in every trait of civilization. It is because religion sanctions and protects the monogamic family that socialism, bent on destroying private property, and the family as its cause, hates and antagonizes religion also. We do not reach the heart of social problems until we realize the inseparable connection between property, the family, and religion, alike threatened by socialism, their common foe. As long as Christianity endures, the monogamic family will endure; as long as the love of a true wife and her children fills the heart of man, private property will be desired and defended as a right, for their sakes. Hence it is that socialists reject every form of Christian overture and alliance.

4. It might be scientifically maintained that monogamy is the natural and normal form of sexual union, because it is the last term in the order of evolution, unless development should return to lower and abandoned forms and become retrogressive. This is a

sufficient answer to the evolutionist. It might also
be argued from the numerical equilibrium of the
sexes, the proportion of men and women being substantially equal. But there is no scientific reason for
abandoning the idea of the family as absolute from
the beginning, commencing as a primeval monogamy,
from which degenerate races have fallen away. This
doctrine which is taught in the Scriptures still underlies all the great works on jurisprudence and is confirmed by Sir Henry Maine in his investigations into
ancient law. Even Darwin rejected a universal
primitive promiscuity as represented by Sir John
Lubbock, on the ground that even among the anthro-
poid apes the highest are "strictly monogamous." [12]
The derivation of names and relationship from
the maternal side, adduced by Morgan as evidence of
polyandry, is otherwise explained by the German
anthropologist Peschel, who cites numerous instances
to show the high sense of conjugal fidelity among
tribes where this strange mode of tracing relationship
is in vogue. He also asserts that Bachofen's idea of
a primitive gynæocracy, or maternal headship, can be
proved only by adducing ancient myths of uncertain
date upon which a forced interpretation has been
placed.[13] The evidence upon which the whole
theory of the evolution of the family rests is derived
from the study of the lowest scattered tribes of modern

[12] Darwin's Descent of Man, part iii, chap. xxii, p. 590.
[13] Peschel's Races of Man, pp. 218, 237. Since these lectures were delivered, Prof. J. G. Schurman, of Cornell University, has published an able
critique on the views of McLennan and Morgan in his Ethical Import of
Darwinism, chap. vi.

men, and involves the assumption that their practices are to be regarded as those of primeval times. The prehistoric monogamy of the Aryan races, the wide prevalence of the *patria potestas*, or paternal supremacy, the ancient ancestor-worship of the Chinese and the preservation of ideas of monogamy even among the lowest races, — all render vastly more probable a partial degeneration from a higher type of family than a general primitive promiscuity. Such contributions to this subject as that of Robertson Smith, in his recent work, " Kinship and Marriage in Early Arabia," do not reach back far enough in time to determine the primeval truth. That every age, not excluding the present, has known something of all the possible deviations from the normal marriage relation, is highly probable; and, therefore, the fragmentary evidence which such writers gather with infinite pains cannot solve the problem. A theorist of the fiftieth century might argue with equal cogency from certain facts of our own land and time, that a Christian people once practised polygamy.

III.

1. What has Christianity to say to these speculations? The time of Christ was one in which the earlier Semitic polygamy had been outgrown, though successive polygamy was still tolerated by the extreme laxity of divorce. That toleration of " hardness of heart," which the legislation of Moses permitted without encouraging, the Rabbi Hillel had so far indulged as to grant divorce if the wife burned the food; and

the popular Rabbi Akiba, who is said to have had eighty thousand disciples, allowed the husband to put away his wife when he found one more beautiful, or upon any arbitrary pretext whatever. After the example of Salome, the sister of Herod the Great, who repudiated her Idumean husband, women also initiated divorce, and the Samaritan woman whom Jesus met at the well had had five husbands. Christ opposed the popular teaching in his reply to his questioners. His doctrine gave to the indissoluble union of two persons, which he declared was the divine intention from the beginning, a genuine rehabilitation, and lifted the marriage relation from the low level of mere mutual agreement to the high plane of a religious bond, sealing it for the Christian ages with the precept, "What God hath joined together, let not man put asunder." We have already traced the influence of this new enunciation of the absolute principle of marriage upon the entire Christian world. Whatever difference of opinion there has been upon the essence of it, whether it is a status, a civil contract, a sacrament, or the union of these, there has been no division of doctrine as to the form of marriage taught by Christ, as an essentially permanent relation between one man and one woman, inviolable by all and to be abrogated for one cause only, a schism in the flesh which marriage has made one.

2. The family, therefore, as instituted by the Creator and explained by Christ is not a mere human invention or product of evolution. It consists of a husband, a wife, and their children. It is a primor-

dial society, a social molecule within the greater social organism, through which life is transmitted and the whole normally augmented. The divinity of its origin is as clearly attested by the physical and mental aptitudes of its constituent members as by the words of Scripture. The eloquent Abbe Vidieu thus portrays these aptitudes: "To man God gave power as a sceptre, thus establishing him as the head of the family; but of the tenderness of woman he made another sceptre more gentle and not less potent. To the king he gave justice, to the queen clemency: in the heart of man he put courage, but in the heart of woman that moral energy with which she overcomes suffering. To the one have been confided the keeping and defence of the family; to the other the care of its happiness. While the chief directs the way, sometimes difficult, offering to his companion a support, she, by her tenderness, consoles and fortifies his heart, diffusing joy even in the midst of the tempest; upon the wounds made by the briers and hardness of the road the one pours wine, the other balm. The family and society are put in relation by the man fulfilling the duties of a citizen; woman, in her dwelling, concealing the charms of her virtue and devoting herself to her family, at the same time giving herself to society. Man dominates by reason, woman by goodness; for the divine ray that descends upon each hearthstone, upon the one sheds more of light, upon the other more of love. But between the heart of man and that of woman is an incessant irradiation, a constant interchange of all that is most intimate in human nature, making one soul of these two souls, and recomposing outside of themselves the ray where affections, cares, and joys unite in the person of the child. The family is complete, but duties are increased and deepened, the rôle of each parent is more sharply defined. For the child is the hope of the family and the nation; the child is humanity perpetuating itself, advancing in the way of perfection or retrograding toward the shades of barbarism; it is the alternative between virtue and vice, truth and error, light and darkness, love and hate, wealth and misery, order and chaos, glory and shame, progression and degradation. The child is the fragile and delicate blossom which the wind can bruise and the sun wither; it is the little fledgling which the mother protects with her wing and shelters with its soft warmth; it is in the blossom of all nature the most feeble, the most helpless of beings. It would die without its mother; it is her milk which sustains it; it is her soft hands alone that can touch without bruising its delicate members; her caresses and kisses alone can impart the warmth of life." [14] Its first and continuous need is love, and how shall this be satisfied if the mother does not watch over it with tender solicitude and the father make provision for the material wants of both?

3. The family constitutes an essential part of the moral order. It is within it alone that the best elements of human nature, both ethical and economical, can be found. It brings to fulfillment the life of man

---

[14] L'Abbe Vidieu, Famille et Divorce, chapitre i.

in the duties and responsibilities of paternity. These are at once the factors of material wellbeing and of moral discipline. The indissoluble bond alone can hold man to his duties and perfect in him the industry, the patience, the temperance, the self-sacrifice which condition the completion of his manhood. If he can escape the obligations of marriage at will, he can withdraw from this school of discipline whenever he feels impatient or indolent, and the whole future of the man is lost in vagabondism and self-indulgence. But if marriage is so much for man, what is it for woman? It is at once a guard to her virtue, a field for her affections, a protection to her rights, a vocation for her noblest powers, and an opportunity for her self-realization. It is in the home where love unites two complementary natures that both are brought to perfection. The necessity of compromise, of growing together in the interests of peace, of mutual helpfulness and forbearance, molds the characters of both and wears away the angularities of selfishness. But it is above all for the child that marriage should be permanent. The child needs both father and mother; the firmness and judgment of the one and the gentleness and inspiration of the other. Who can estimate the misfortune of one who has missed the influence of either of these two factors of character? It is like being born without some organ or member of the body. When charity and philanthropy have done their best to realize artificially the conditions of a home in an asylum for orphans, it still seems to us but a dreary place, like a hospital for the sick. How accursed, then, is that social philosophy that would destroy the home, establish free marriage as a rule of society, transfer the care of children to the impersonal guardianship of the State, and render every child an orphan from its birth!

4. A false or superficial interpretation of the New Testament has created the impression in some minds that the Christian idea of marriage is vacillating and contradictory, sometimes commending and sometimes condemning the married state. Nothing can be more clear and harmonious than the teachings of Christ and his apostles when viewed in the light of their special applications. "Marriage," says the writer to the Hebrews, "is honourable in all." Paul, in his First Letter to Timothy, rebukes those who forbid to marry, and exhorts "younger women" to "marry, bear children, guide the house." And yet there were circumstances under which the rule could not be wisely applied. In times of calamity and danger he dissuaded from marriage, though even in those trying times marriage was not represented as a sin. The wedded state might also interfere with spiritual duty. When pleasing one's wife prevented pleasing the Lord, when the love of wife and children restrained men from the public committment of themselves to Christian faith, when wedlock endangered the unequal yoking together of Christians and Pagans, with a divided household, Paul counseled against marriage. There is no reason for thinking that he would not display the same conservative and prudent spirit

to-day. It is not the number of children added to society, but the number of healthy, well-reared, and well-trained children that increases human happiness, social prosperity, and moral life. The constitutionally feeble, the diseased, the pauperized, the incapable, those who cannot provide for the wants of a family, ought certainly not to marry. While Christianity places no moral virtue in celibacy in itself, it honors a voluntary singleness of life, devoted to high moral and spiritual aims. The enforced celibacy of the clergy is a perversion of Christian teaching, without apostolic warrant in either precept or example. It is a sufficient refutation of the Romish theory that the apostle whom it honors as the first primate of the Church is the one whom we certainly know to have been a married man.

IV.

The union of persons in the family is the ground of certain rights, because it controls and modifies that unfolding of powers and capacities which underlies all other rights as the root of all. Christianity affects society by its teachings concerning these ethical relations, and therefore enters most influentially into the solution of social problems.

1. When a child is born into the world it is not with its own consent, and its relation to its parents is not one of contract, but one of status. What does the status of a child imply? As a moral being it will in time be capable of duty. It is by nature morally free — a person. But personality, with its attributes

of obligation to duty and moral freedom, implies rights as the essential conditions of self-realization. The child's first right is to support. Its second right is to instruction and training that will fit it for the performance of duty. These rights are self-evident, like the laborer's right to the fruit of his labor. But every right implies a correlative duty. Whose duty is it to support and instruct the child? Not primarily the duty of the State, for the State has not been consulted upon the question of its being. If the State were to determine the conditions of marriage and the number of offspring it would be otherwise. If ever a society should exist in which the duties of support and education should be assumed by the State, it would assuredly claim the correlative rights that are involved in this obligation. But the child's existence is owing to parental, not social action; and therefore the duty of its sustenance and training falls upon its parents. And here two important principles emerge into light: first, that the parents are morally responsible for the welfare and culture of their child, and culpable if they have not made provision for the discharge of their duties; and second, that they themselves, though their marriage is at first a contract, have entered into a status and created a status for their child which they cannot voluntarily dissolve. The bearing of this upon divorce is evident, but for the present let us consider its relation to inheritance. The right of heirship is maintained throughout the Scriptures and is inseparably connected with the idea of the family as divinely instituted. The historical researches of Sir Henry Maine have demonstrated that inheritance is a universally recognized right, natural and fundamental, indissolubly connected with filiation, and equitably terminable only for a specific cause.[15] Testamentary law, authorizing the disposition of property by will, and primogeniture, the exclusive inheritance of the eldest son, are late and artificial additions to early custom, wholly unknown to our German and English forefathers until the first was borrowed from Roman jurisprudence and the second was introduced by feudalism. The right of making a will is sometimes used by paternal ambition to perpetuate a family name or to secure property from being wasted, without regard to the interest of the disinherited; and primogeniture, happily not borrowed by us from the English law, is certainly a perversion of natural right. Testamentary law was invented, as its history shows, to secure, and not to limit, inheritance. A wholly unwarranted interference is now seriously proposed by certain speculative minds in the form of a legal limitation of inheritance, fixing by law the maximum of property which may be transmitted by a father to his children. No device could be more arbitrary, absurd, or inequitable. Arbitrary, because no rule can be discovered for fixing this maximum. Absurd, because every father would evade it by transferring his property during his lifetime. Inequitable, because it disregards the status into which a child is born and which it has been the object of his father's life to create for his child as

[15] Maine's Ancient Law, chap. vi.

well as for himself. It is frequently contended that, though we may admit the validity of the right of private property during its possessor's lifetime, the right is extinguished by his death; but here it is forgotten that testamentary disposition is the act of a living man, not a dead one, and that the property of an intestate is a part of the status of his family who survive him, created by him for them while invested with proprietorship. When it is remembered that the love of children is usually the strongest motive in the production and conservation of wealth, it is evident that this species of robbery is as devoid of justice as any other socialistic subterfuge for the destruction of proprietary rights. It is the glory of Christianity that, as Sir Henry Maine has said, "it has always maintained the sanctity of wills." The right of inheritance is a fundamental postulate of Christian theology. "If a son, then an heir," reasons the great apostle. There is no nobler impulse than that which prompts a father by the toil, prudence, and self-sacrifice of his own life to offer to his children advantages which he himself has never known.

2. The family is a corporation initiated by contract but terminating in a status. It is a moral status whose purpose is fulfilled, not in the birth and training of children, but in moral love. Marriage, considered as a contract merely, scarcely rises above the dignity of concubinage. Children are not so much the purpose as the blessing of wedlock, for otherwise unfruitfulness alone would be a sufficient ground of

divorce. If marriage is a moral status, what is woman's position in it? No doubt it partly depends upon the usage and customs of a particular time and place, for in entering marriage she knows the status she may expect. But what, ideally, and in the Christian sense, is the status of a married woman? It is not a complete subordination of herself and extinction of her moral personality by absorption into the personality of her husband. She still has rights and duties and does not cease to be both free and responsible. She is in no sense a slave. It is from that condition that Christian marriage has emancipated her. Her rôle is "obedience," but only "in the Lord." The moral law, or law of God, intrenches her and constitutes her defence. Her husband cannot rightly compel her to disregard it, and she is for herself the judge of its applications. The union is a completely ethical one, for to her duty to obey is correlated her right to be loved. "Husbands, love your wives," is as imperative as, "Wives, be obedient to your husbands." Marriage is a subordination of the wife to the leadership of her husband, but cannot be a renunciation of personality. She has rights. She may think and believe and even act contrary to her husband's direction. Has she also a right to independent property? This must depend upon the premarital contract, for marriage is a union of persons, not an annihilation of preëxisting rights, which the wife may choose to retain. In our Christian States this right is now generally conceded. The wisdom and justice of merging her property with her husband's estate must be determined by specific circumstances. Her natural right to a share of her husband's property is very clear. As co-producer of his wealth and as dependent upon him by her subordination in family life, she is evidently entitled to support and inheritance. Otherwise she would often lose the fruits of her labors. "The provision for the widow," says Sir Henry Maine, "was attributable to the exertions of the Church, which never relaxed its solicitude for the interest of wives surviving their husbands, winning, perhaps, one of the most arduous of its triumphs when, after exacting for two or three centuries an express promise from the husband at marriage to endow his wife, it at length succeeded in engrafting the principle of dower on the customary law of all western Europe."[16] Within fifty years the legal status of married women has wholly changed. Under the common law, the family was a legal unit, represented by the husband. Under modern statutes, in most of our American States, it is now a legal duality, in which two distinct legal persons are recognized. Husband and wife are co-equal partners, with certain immunities on the side of the wife and certain liabilities on the side of the husband. She can sequester all of her property and claim complete support from her husband for herself and her children. Within the period from 1860 to 1878, under this *régime*, in Massachusetts marriages increased only four per cent., divorces more than one hundred per cent., and population forty-five per

---

[16] Maine, op. cit., chap. vii.

cent., showing that marriages are relatively decreasing and divorces increasing at an enormous rate. The new laws have been associated with new industrial employments for women. In 1840 only seven occupations were open to women. In 1883 there were nearly three hundred.[17] Connected with these legal and industrial changes are the boarding-house life, the factory-girl slavery, and the shop-girl bondage of our decade, with their temptations and hardships. Marriage tends to be regarded as a sexual partnership, to which the home is unnecessary, children are an impediment, and divorce is a frequent termination. Professor Ely reports that in a single New England factory-town of thirty thousand inhabitants, he found two hundred couples living together outside the bonds of wedlock. For all these evils, only too real and too serious, connected with a practical Malthusianism, involving both vice and crime, Christianity has a remedy. It is the old one offered by Paul: "Let the younger women marry, bear children, guide the house."

3. The spirit of our times favors the further "emancipation" of woman, but it is well to be sure in what her true emancipation consists before giving reinforcement to the ranks of the radicals. The next stadium in the proposed programme of progress is the legal establishment of woman's political personality. I do not see how it can be logically withheld from unmarried women who have reached the years of majority and are self-supporting. The

[17] The Married Woman's Statutes, by Jonathan Smith, p. 10.

reason for withholding suffrage does not lie in sex, but in the family. The Christian idea of marriage precludes the universal suffrage of women. A family is normally represented through its responsible head. That head, according to the Christian as well as the historic conception, is the husband and father. If the wife is clothed with political power, she has every right with her husband. She must then bear the burden equally of every duty. This involves a divided responsibility for the wellbeing of the family. She must use her property for the support of herself, her children, and her husband, as he now must use his. It is but simple justice. Most married women will prefer their present condition to this double headship. To invest wives with political sovereignty is to divide the household and to introduce into the married state a new cause of disputation and disruption. It destroys that unity which is the first essential to an ideal family life.

4. There remains but little time in which to speak of the dissolution of marriage. It is the less necessary in this presence, because the Christian doctrine on that subject has been admirably expounded in the lucid and conclusive little volume by President Hovey on "The Scripture Law of Divorce." There is but one cause for which the dissolution of the marriage bond can be granted, according to the law of Christ. Separation, temporary or permanent, however, is a proper alternative to continued marital relations when the ends of human existence cannot otherwise be attained. The Christian Church is

bound absolutely by this high ideal and it is the duty of all men to aim at its realization. As Dr. Hovey says: "Civil governments sometimes find it impracticable to make their laws touching divorce agree precisely with the divine law. The wickedness of the people may forbid this. Yet the more nearly those laws can be brought to the evangelical standard, and properly executed, the more useful will they be to the people. And it is difficult to overestimate the educational power of civil laws, and the importance of bringing them into perfect accord with the true principles of morality."[18] It is good legal ground that the nature of wedlock implies its perpetuity for life, and this is always assumed by at least one of the contracting parties. "Eternity," says Dr. Paul Janet, "so truly enters into the nature of love, that love would not venture to ask anything, or to grant anything without promising eternity. Its first acts are always oaths of fidelity without end, and even when it practises deception, it is obliged to use feigned words, or it would obtain nothing. It is urged that the heart has rights, and that vows of eternity are impossible. I acknowledge that love has rights for the forming of the conjugal union, but it has none for dissolving it. To the principle of the heart's liberty we must oppose that of the heart's fidelity; and herein we assign to it an office more beautiful, and a glory more pure, than if we claimed for it the privilege of giving itself up to chance and of changing its office without ceasing. I confess

[18] The Scriptural Doctrine of Divorce, by Alvah Hovey, D.D., pp. 72, 73.

that to require of the heart an attachment which cannot be given up demands grave reasons. I discern two such reasons, which appear to me to be irrefutable : the dignity of the wife and the interest of the children." [19]

[19] Janet, La Famille, pp. 300, 303.

VI.

CHRISTIANITY AND THE PROBLEMS OF EDUCATION.

CHRISTIANITY AND THE PROBLEMS OF EDUCATION.

I. EDUCATION AS A SOCIAL FUNCTION.
   1. Unconscious and Conscious Education.
   2. Oriental Education.
   3. Classical Education.

II. CHRISTIANITY AS AN EDUCATING POWER.
   1. The Christian Conception of Education.
   2. The Historic Influence of Christianity.
   3. The Cultural Breadth of Christianity.
   4. The Triumphs of Christian Culture.
   5. Commenius and Milton.

III. CHRISTIANITY AND CONTEMPORARY EDUCATION.
   1. Sciolism in Pedagogics.
   2. The Attack on Religion in the Schools.
   3. The Relation of Christianity to our Schools.
       (1) Ours a Christian Nation.
       (2) Our Higher Education Christian.
       (3) The Theorists Commend Religion in Education.
   4. The Secularization of the Schools.
   5. The Cause of this Secularization.
   6. Conclusions:
       (1) The State cannot impart a Complete Education.
       (2) The Family and the Church must complete Education.
       (3) Christian Teachers must do their Duty.

VI.

CHRISTIANITY AND THE PROBLEMS OF EDUCATION.

I.

1. THE unfolding of a human being, like the growth of a plant, depends largely upon its surroundings. What soil, air, and sunshine are to the plant, family influence, social customs, and public opinion are to the child. Long before conscious purposes of human development were formed education existed; for the imitative instinct in the presence of unreflecting example is sufficient to call into action many of the human faculties. A continuity of life runs through all human history and our education began before we were born. The principle of heredity extends not only to organic descent, but also to intellectual and moral development. Language, literature, law, and science constitute a veritable inheritance. Each generation may begin where its predecessor ended, but only on the condition of some organizing effort to acquaint the young with the history and acquisitions of the past. This, however, even very crude peoples undertake and accomplish. Ideals of human life, consciously or unconsciously, are formed in the mind, and these become the educational types of different ages and nations. At last they are gathered

in a conscious purpose. Institutions are then created to mold the young after these ideals, and thus education comes to be a social function.

To educate a child is to enable it to fulfil its life-plan and realize its destiny. Organized educational work involves the clear conception of an end to be attained, the conscious apprehension in clear-cut form of the child's nature and future. Every people advanced beyond the rudimentary condition of savagery has such an idea of the end to which education furnishes the means. "The national education," says Dr. Barnard, "is at once a cause and an effect of the national character; and accordingly the history of education affords the only ready and perfect key to the history of the human race and of each nation in it — an unfailing standard for estimating its advance or retreat upon the line of human progress."[1]

2. Among the oriental nations the individual counts for nothing. His destination is a place in a complex, stationary, and completed social framework, and his education is shaped with the end of adjusting him to his place. In China the mind looks backward, never forward, and the type of culture may be called ancestral. Every human being is taught to be like his fathers, to reverence them as deities, and all personal spontaneity is rigorously repressed. The caste discipline of India is similar in its retrospective tendency, training every child, according to the one of the four castes to which he belongs by birth, to take the place of his forefathers. Persian education is built upon

[1] Quoted in Painter's History of Education, introduction.

the stability of the State, and service to the sovereign is the end of all endeavor. The ancient Hebrews molded the young upon a theocratic pattern more elevated and noble than any other oriental conception, shaping the entire life for service to God, and thus placing the moral development above the intellectual.

3. The classical nations of antiquity regarded the State as the end of existence, the individual as the means of its strength and perpetuity. They differed from the oriental peoples in conceiving the high development of the individual as a desirable object, but only as subsidiary to the ulterior purpose of glorifying public life. The Greek and Roman theories of education — the martial training of Lycurgus, the æsthetic culture of Pythagoras, the dialectic practice of the Sophists, the philosophic politics of Cicero, and the rhetorical system of Quintilian — all contemplate the preparation of the few for whom these phases of education were designed for the public duties of citizenship. Nowhere in antiquity, nowhere outside of Christendom, do we find the full and harmonious development of man *for his own sake* regarded as the end of education.

II.

1. With the advent of Christianity a new conception entered the minds of men. It was not distinctly formulated either by the Founder of Christianity himself or by any of his chosen apostles, but its germ was latent in the new idea of man.

"Be ye perfect," said Jesus, "even as your Father in heaven is perfect." At first this perfection was understood as a moral perfection, a growth in righteousness. But reflection has developed this new idea into a vastly broader and more symmetrical one. It was much to conceive of man as capable of any form of perfection and to place this before him as a goal to be attained by every individual. Holiness is wholeness. Slowly but logically the conception has grown into the modern Christian ideal of education. Not only moral character but intellectual power belongs to that Being in whose image man is created. The realization of man's complete nature as the image of God involves his growth of mind, his perception of plan and wisdom in the creation of the world. Each day should add some new lesson in the divine tuition. As a son of God, study becomes to him a part of worship. "To know, in order to be," is the new maxim of Christian faith.

2. We must not forget, however, that this now familiar contemporary idea is recent and has a history that has led to doubt concerning the attitude of Christianity toward certain forms of culture. In the early centuries of the era which it has created, Christianity claimed no alliance with the intellectual forces of the world and introduced no scientific renaissance. Its primary work was moral and spiritual, and this required other instruments than mental culture. Its next task was the humanizing of the Northern barbarians, whose multitudes were brought

to the standard of the cross by moral object-lessons rather than by a scientific process. The time was not ripe for the unfolding of those resources of knowledge that lay concealed, awaiting the preparation of the nations for their discovery and utilization. The first need of the world was a moral regeneration. This Christianity gave. The next was the refining and civilizing of the Northern races. This also Christianity supplied amid the ruins of the Roman Empire. It did it through those schools, now scoffed at as barren and unproductive, in which the intellect of Europe was drilled in the processes of dialectic, and rendered capable of logical analysis. It was a needed schooling, the only one the age could bear. Then followed the training in the old humanities, the opening and exposition of the ancient classics, lost books to the lands that produced them, new books to the races of the North, at the period of the revival of letters. Finally, the trained and sharpened intellect was turned toward nature, whose great banquet board of truth lay all untouched, ready for the eager appetite. The modern sciences became the food of the robust mind, made powerful and agile in the palæstra of scholasticism. "The past," says Emerson, in rebuke of the modern scoffers, "has baked your loaf, and in the strength of its bread you would break up the oven." "Not a man in Europe now," as John Henry Newman reminds us, and he might have said in America also, "who talks bravely against the Church, but owes it to the Church that he can talk at all."

There are two co-equal elements in true human education: discipline and instruction. Christianity has neglected neither. The first requisite in every person's training is moral discipline. That was Christianity's first gift to the world. It trained men to reverence and love truth, to suffer for it, to die for it. The next need is power of analysis. This was given in the much-abused scholasticism. The rude nations of the North had known nothing like it. It was to them what a problem in algebra is to a modern plowboy, a lesson of priceless value, though the answer itself may be unimportant. Then comes the need of information. The past rose up to instruct men through the lips of Homer and Plato, Cicero and Cæsar. But the present also required a voice. The past supplied a language. Astrology becomes astronomy, alchemy becomes chemistry, geology and biology and the other newborn sciences appear. What are they, all of them, but the facts of nature poured into the molds of logic which scholasticism had prepared; their very names, the "ologies," signifying the special logics?

3. It cannot be truly said that Christianity has been the foe of knowledge.[2] It has preserved what

---

[2] Those who have read Draper's History of the Conflict between Religion and Science may feel disposed to question this statement. It should be remembered that I use "Christianity" as a synonym with "the influence of Jesus," not as equivalent to the historical Church. The spirit of Jesus is expressed in his words: "Ye shall know the truth, and the truth shall make you free" (John 8: 32). While Christians have not always welcomed truth which seemed to them contradictory of truth already accepted, and, therefore, falsehood, the spirit of Christ, whenever it has really moved men to know the truth, and has broadened their minds sufficiently to receive it, has

antiquity possessed, and prepared for and incited to what the present has discovered. It must be admitted, however, that it places moral before intellectual development, but who that reflects will not? "Seek ye first the kingdom of heaven," said our Lord, but immediately added, "and all these things" — the necessities of human life on its loftiest as well as on its lowest plane — "shall be added unto you." Asceticism, it is true, was abnormally developed in the early Church. It cultivated a spirit of "other-worldliness," as George Eliot calls it, repressing the body and its pleasures, and creating a hatred of the world. Such was not the spirit of Jesus or his immediate disciples. They overcame the world, indeed, but not by destroying it. Their triumph was a moral victory, not a physical extinction. Christ came eating and drinking; he sought the companionship of men; he honored marriage and maintained the sacredness of family life; he blessed the little children, and taught his disciples to trace the presence of God in nature; he prayed in his last recorded petition for his own, not that they might

opened their sympathies for real knowledge of all kinds. As a distinguished student and teacher of history has said in a valuable work on this subject. "The work of Christianity has been mighty indeed. Through these two thousand years, despite the waste of its energies on all the things its blessed Founder most earnestly condemned, — on fetich and subtlety and war and pomp, — it has undermined servitude, mitigated tyranny, given hope to the hopeless, comfort to the afflicted, light to the blind, bread to the starving, joy to the dying, and this work continues. And its work for science, too, has been great. It has fostered science often. Nay, it has nourished that feeling of self-sacrifice for human good, which has nerved some of the bravest men for these battles." — The Warfare of Science, by Andrew D. White, LL.D.

be taken out of the world, but that they might be kept from the evil. If Tertullian and Chrysostom and Jerome condemned all intercourse with the world and all seeking after natural knowledge, others, as Basil, for example, warmly commended culture. "We ought to be armed with every resource, and to this end the reading of poets, historians, and orators is very useful," says Basil.[3] Charlemagne wisely wrote: "Although it is better to do than to know, yet it is necessary to know, in order to be able to do. ... Hence we admonish you not to neglect the study of the sciences."[4] Throughout the history of our era we trace the affinity of the Christianized mind for every noble form of knowledge; and yet it must be confessed that Christianity everywhere gives the first place to personal righteousness.

4. If the perfection of the Christian idea of education seems the result of a slow development, it forms no exception to the general law of growth. Christianity has had to deal with men as it found them. It has converted pagans into Christians, barbarians into scholars, dialecticians into scientists. If an ecclesiastical hierarchy at Rome has impeded rather than advanced the progress of human knowledge, it is not because it has been fettered by any doctrines of Christ, but because it has been governed by a self-centred conservatism. The "Holy Roman Empire" was as distinctly a human creation as the Empire of

---

[3] Quoted by Painter, op. cit. p. 99.
[4] Quoted by Painter, op. cit. p. 105.

the Cæsars. Papal obstructiveness to scientific progress has been a purely strategic policy prompted by the instinct of self-preservation. It has ignominiously failed, though Christianity itself has triumphed. Of all the intellectual influences that have ever appeared in history, Christianity alone has matured its fruit. Arabian learning was, indeed, brilliant, but proved short-lived. It lacked the element of intellectual vitality — consecration to truth. It appealed to the sword instead of to the soul of man, and perished by the sword it had unsheathed. Romanism has proved retrogressive and incapable of leading civilization, because it has been wanting in faith. Professing exclusive authority from God, it has feared to trust the reason and conscience which God placed in man for the study of God's world. Its last and losing battle has been in the struggle to confine the mind to the study of those " humanities " which in the beginning it treated with distrust, the classic writings of paganism. It has resisted that naturalism which prompted the scientific movement and pervades the intellectual training of to-day. It has staked all on the ridiculous tenet that heathen classics are more compatible with Christian faith and life than communion with God's works in the realm of nature. Even Protestantism has but slowly and reluctantly broken from the chain of tradition that held men to merely verbal study; but, following its better lights, it has cast the chain aside, and the investigation of nature is now led, as it should be, by Christian men.

5. It was the gentle pastor Commenius who, in

the seventeenth century, put in final phrase the Christian ideal of education. "Education," he says, "is a development of the whole man." A Christian poet, John Milton, in the same age, phrased the doctrine thus: "The end, then, of learning is to repair the ruins of our first parents by regaining to know God aright, and out of that knowledge to love him, to imitate him, to be like him, as we may the nearest by possessing our souls of virtue, which, being united to the heavenly grace of faith, makes up the highest perfection. But because our understanding cannot in this body found itself but on sensible things, nor arrive so clearly to the knowledge of God and things invisible, as by orderly conning over the visible and inferior creature, the same method is necessarily to be followed in all discreet teaching. And seeing every nation affords not experience and tradition enough for all kinds of learning, therefore we are chiefly taught the languages of those people who have at any time been most industrious after wisdom; so that language is but the instrument conveying to us things useful to be known. And though a linguist should pride himself to have all the tongues that Babel cleft the world into, yet if he have not studied the solid things themselves, as well as the words and lexicons, he were nothing so much to be esteemed a learned man as any yeoman or tradesman competently wise in his mother dialect only."[5] This remarkable passage at once sets forth, in its quaint fashion, both the end and the method of true educa-

[5] Milton's Tractate on Education.

tion, acknowledging the equal claims of the humanities and the sciences; and may be regarded as the most succinct and satisfactory judgment that has yet been uttered on the philosophy of human development.

III.

1. We are living in a time when the abstract idea of education exercises more influence over the minds of men than it has ever exercised before in the history of the world. Ours is an age in which faith in dynamic agencies is boundless. "Change," "Progress," "Evolution," are the watchwords of the hour. And yet a thoughtful investigator discovers more doubt, antagonism, and contradiction among educational theorists and their disciples among teachers than any other age reveals. Ends, means, and methods the most opposite are lauded and applied, sometimes as new and final discoveries, and almost always in the name of "science." It is an age of sciolists. As soon as anything calls itself a "science," it has authority. The mind of the moderns has a special reverence for the "practical" also. But the sphere of practice is very dimly outlined. Chemistry, for example, is usually praised as a "practical" study and moral philosophy is regarded as less "practical;" notwithstanding the fact that there are but few instances in the life of the average man when a personal knowledge of chemical science is strictly necessary, while moral conduct, as Matthew Arnold says, "is three fourths of life." It is regarded "practical" to name all the bones in the human body, while the

study of an oration of Cicero's would not be so esteemed; and yet one is called upon to make a speech more often than to give the scientific name of any anatomical part.

2. A schoolbook on science is considered obsolete if it does not contain last year's discoveries; and yet precepts and doctrines that have been slowly verified in the experience of centuries are arbitrarily excluded from our schoolrooms. It is generally admitted that the principles of Christianity have led the world's advancement, and yet it would be hazardous for the author of a textbook designed for our public schools to say so. The principle governing the first grant of public lands for purposes of education, in 1785, was stated: "Religion, morality, and knowledge being necessary to good government and the happiness of mankind, schools and the means of education shall be forever encouraged."[6] See what a change a century has made. "That is my 'Political Economy,' said a Christian college president, "prepared for high-schools and colleges. I sent it the other day to one of our state superintendents of education; but it was returned to me with the note that its first sentence condemned it for use in public schools." That first sentence was: "The source of all wealth is the beneficence of God."[7] A series of geographies, accurate in details, revised to date, and beautifully printed, was rejected by the school board of Chicago

---

[6] Quoted by Painter, op. cit. p. 316.

[7] This case and the following one are reported by the late A. A. Hodge, D.D., in the New Princeton Review for January, 1887, p. 29.

after having been in use a year, *because these books recognized the existence of God.* It was only ten years ago that Dr. Woolsey wrote, in his Political Science: "We have not yet quite reached the extreme that the teacher must never mention God to children's ears, but it must logically come, if modern unbelief is to have the career that many look for."[8] The logic of events has confirmed the logic of this unwelcome prediction, and in less than a decade it has been fulfilled.

3. This change has come about, notwithstanding three considerations, which separately, but much more together, ought to have rendered it impossible: (1) ours is a Christian nation; (2) the superior education of this country has been chiefly in the hands of Christian teachers, in schools founded by Christian men, with an increasing percentage of Christian students; and (3) the general opinion of educational philosophers is that morality and religion are desirable and necessary elements in human education.

(1) Justice Shea maintains that while the Constitution of the United States does not formally recognize the existence of God or set forth any legislative profession of faith, "its entire context and the laws in pursuance thereof, like the form of that more ancient Saxon government upon which ours was molded, declare, with approved wisdom and decorum, by necessary presupposition and inference, that the tenets of the Christian religion lie at the foundations

---

[8] Woolsey's Political Science, vol. ii, p. 414.

of the government and are to protect and regulate its operations." [9]

Daniel Webster, in interpreting the national Constitution, says: "There is nothing we look for with more certainty than the principle that Christianity is a part of the law of the land — general, tolerant Christianity, independent of sects and parties." [10] Kent and Story have held the same doctrine and the courts have repeatedly embodied the principle. And yet a nation whose Constitution was devised by men who, at Franklin's suggestion, began their deliberations with prayer to God; the session of whose national Congress is opened regularly with prayer; whose armies and navies are provided with Christian chaplains paid from the public treasury to conduct religious exercises; whose magistrates are sworn into office in the name and presence of God, and by kissing the Book the sanctity of which seals the solemnity of the oath, and whose judicial action is based on the validity of sworn testimony, — such a nation has in public office men who reject schoolbooks *because* they contain the name of God, and carefully guard the future citizen from all mention and knowledge of the Being in whose name the most solemn acts of citizenship are by law required to be performed.

(2) Not only is this a Christian nation in its traditions and legal implications, but in its essence and development. That the nation was founded by

---

[9] George Shea's The Nature and Form of the American Government Founded in the Christian Religion, p. 13.
[10] Quoted by Dr. A. A. Hodge, loc. cit.

Christian men does not need even to be asserted. The growth of Christianity in the United States from 1800 to 1880 exceeded its growth in the entire world during the first eight centuries after Christ, although it was accepted as a state religion by the Roman Empire in the fourth century of its era. Notwithstanding the enormous addition of heterogeneous and non-Christian elements by immigration, excluding now the Roman Catholic growth, the relative increase of evangelical Christians alone is something impressive. According to Dr. Dorchester, in the eighty years from the beginning of our century to 1880, when the last census was taken, the evangelical communicants in the United States increased from one in every fifteen to one in every five inhabitants. The increase of ministers has been nearly as rapid and that of church organizations even more rapid. In these eighty years the evangelical communicants have increased three times as rapidly as the entire population. The educational work shows equally surprising progress. The property of denominational colleges was, in 1880, three times as great as that of all non-denominational colleges together, including those founded by the State. Four fifths of all the collegiate students in the country, in 1880, were in denominational colleges. The increase of these colleges was five times that of the non-denominational. The increase of students in them was more than five times that in the non-denominational. While population increased fourfold, denominational colleges and the students in them increased nearly eightfold, or nearly twice as rapidly as population.[11] And yet it is considered an objection to a textbook for use in our public schools if it contains the name of the Deity.

(3) Now let us pass from these tedious figures to ask if the authorities on the science of education counsel this exclusion of religion. I take down from the shelves of my library the six best known and most reputable works on education in my possession and quote the first words upon which my eye falls relating to the subject. First, let us listen to Horace Mann, who, as the author and defender of the public school system in our country, is entitled to be heard. He says: "Our system earnestly inculcates all Christian morals; it founds its morality on a basis of religion; it welcomes the religion of the Bible. . . . I could not avoid regarding the man who should oppose the religious education of the young as an insane man."[12] A most distinguished French writer, Paroz, says: "We can say of those who would banish Christ from education and the school what St. Paul said of the hostile Jews, that they are the enemies of the human race."[13] A celebrated German authority, Karl Schmidt, in speaking of the doctrines of Jesus, writes: "This is absolute truth, doctrine for all time, in the appropriation and realization of which lies the task of mankind."[14] Another German writer, Rosen-

---

[11] These statistics are taken from Dr. Daniel Dorchester's The Problem of Religious Progress.

[12] Horace Mann, "On Religious Education," in Massachusetts Reports.

[13] Paroz, Histoire Universelle de la Pédagogie.

[14] Schmidt, Geschichte der Pädagogik, which Painter says "is probably the ablest work that has yet been written on educational history."

kranz, of whose book it has been said that "it alone justifies its philosophy of education by an appeal to psychology and history," assigns to religion three educational ends: "(1) consecration; (2) the initiation of the youth into the forms of worship as found in some particular religion, and (3) his reconciliation with his lot."[15] If it be thought that these last citations express foreign rather than the best American ideas upon the subject, we can find no better known authority than Dr. W. T. Harris, who says: "Faith is a secular virtue as well a theological virtue, and whosoever teaches another view of the world . . . teaches a doctrine subversive of faith in this peculiar sense, and also subversive of man's life in all that makes it worth living."[16] One might expect to find a different view in Herbert Spencer's work on "Education," but we read: "The discipline of science is superior to that of our ordinary education, because of the religious culture that it gives." Is Spencer also among the prophets? "Doubtless," he adds, "in much of the science that is current, there is a pervading spirit of irreligion; but not in that true science, which has passed beyond the superficial into the profound."[17] Then follows a quotation from Professor Huxley, too excellent and pertinent to be omitted: "True science and true religion are twin-sisters, and the separation of either from the other is sure to prove the death of both. Science prospers exactly in

[15] Rosenkranz, The Philosophy of Education (Brackett's translation).
[16] Quoted by Dr. Hodge from the Journal of Social Science, May, 1884.
[17] Spencer's Education: Intellectual, Moral, and Physical, p. 90.

proportion as it is religious; and religion flourishes in exact proportion to the scientific depth and firmness of its basis. The great deeds of philosophers have been less the fruit of their intellect than of the direction of that intellect by an eminently religious tone of mind. Truth has yielded herself rather to their patience, their love, their single-heartedness, and their self-denial, than to their logical acumen." [18]

Is it not something anomalous that a people whose common law is pervaded with Christianity, among whom voluntary adhesion to that faith has lately increased beyond all precedent, should witness among themselves a secularization of education so absolute as to drive from the schools that religion which the greatest authorities on the training of the mind consider essential to its completeness, and which even the most radical scientific philosophers of our age have esteemed as a twin-sister of science itself? Let us first correctly apprehend the fact, then inquire into its cause, and if possible discover a method of final rectification.

4. "The manifest tendency of the time," says Professor Payne, of the University of Michigan, "is toward the secularization of the school. The modern State has become an educator and relegates religious instruction to the family and the Church." [19] It is a "tendency" rather than a realized condition, of which

---

[18] Quoted by Herbert Spencer immediately after the sentence just quoted from him.

[19] Payne's Contributions to the Science of Education, Essay on The Secularization of the School.

this writer speaks, but it is one of rapid growth. In the New England States this secularization has not proceeded so far as in the West. In Massachusetts the daily reading of a portion of the Bible is commanded by law, but there is a "conscience clause" for objectors. In Ohio the Bible is excluded from the public schools under a decision of the Supreme Court. In Wisconsin it is an offence punishable with a fine for a teacher to give any religious instruction in the public schools. In the high school of Milwaukee materialism is said to be openly taught. In a land where no high office can be entered upon without a solemn oath in the presence of God, it is legal to deny that he governs the universe or even has existence, but illegal to assert the reality of his being. Could Washington have dreamed of such a state of public opinion, when he said: "Reason and experience both forbid us to expect that national morality can prevail in exclusion of religious principles"?[20]

5. What is the cause of the growing secularization of the schools? It is not any incompatibility of our Constitution with Christianity, it is not the decadence of Christian faith or the relative diminution of Christians, it is not the conclusion of high authorities that religion is detrimental to the child. All this has been clearly shown. Nor is it the opposition of Romanists to the use of a Protestant version of the Bible. A prominent Catholic newspaper condemns the exclusion of the Bible from the public schools of

[20] Washington's Farewell Address.

Cincinnati and adds: "To us godless schools are still less acceptable than sectarian schools, and we object less to the reading of King James's Bible, even in the schools, than we do to the exclusion of all religious instruction. Even Protestantism of the orthodox stamp is far less evil than German infidelity."[21] What then is the cause of this growing secularization? Professor Payne states it thus: "Education has become, or is rapidly becoming, a function of the State. . . . With the State as educator, the school becomes a civil institution, and as such it must abandon religious instruction, which must be relegated to the family and the Church." And yet he goes on to say that "the public school must teach morality, because morality is an element of good citizenship." Mr. M. J. Savage puts the case very vigorously. He says: "The State has no right to set itself up as a life insurance organization concerning eternity. It is none of the business of the government whether my soul goes to one place in the next world or the other. The State should concern itself as to how I behave myself as a citizen of this world; and there its jurisdiction ends."[22] The cause of the secularization of the schools seems to be the idea that religion is no part of the State's function. We must distinguish between recognition and affirmation. The organic law of our nation and of the several states *recognizes* religion and offers it protection, but does not *affirm* it. It may, therefore, *permit* religion

---

[21] The New York Tablet, quoted by Payne, loc. cit.
[22] Savage's Social Problems, article Common School Education.

to be taught, but cannot *teach* it. The State, as a state, cannot teach religion, because teaching involves a choice between doctrines which the State is not empowered to make.[23]

6. From this position we may draw three conclusions : (1) The State cannot impart a complete education. If the Christian conception of it as the development of the whole man is the true one, an ideal education is beyond the reach of the State. The State has no theory of manhood, only one of citizenship. Even this has been crude enough. It has given us a system of public schools of great value, but very imperfectly adapted to its own end of producing citizens. The industrial side of development has been left almost entirely out of sight. The result is that we have a top-heavy system whose fruits are now beginning to be harvested and they prove bitter fruits. The old system of apprenticeship has passed away. We have millions of boys with the habits and tastes of school-boys but without the skill and industry of self-supporting workers. Our skilled workmen have to be imported. The learned professions are overcrowded. Clerks and small traders crowd one another in a destructive competition. The education imparted by our public school system is

[23] It is certainly contrary to the spirit of our national Constitution " to require compulsory support, by taxation or otherwise, of religious instruction ; " and, as Judge Cooley says (Constitutional Limitations), is " not lawful under any of the American constitutions." But it is equally clear that the exclusion of a book, provided it cannot be proved injurious, or of a teacher, provided he merely expresses his own views, from a school supported by the State, *on account of a religious doctrine which is not sectarian*, is a religious persecution.

literary and commercial. It often unfits its recipients for the positions open to them, making them scorn the labor of their hands and seek to support themselves by their wits. Such education simply intensifies the social problem, instead of solving it. It tends to produce superficial and conceited men and women instead of self-supporting and substantial members of society. The great need of our public school system is the introduction of industrialism into its programme of development. The State certainly has an interest and a duty in educating those who cannot be otherwise educated: the orphan, the waif, the outcast, the pauper; it may be expedient also for those otherwise circumstanced to be intrusted to the public schools, but the whole system needs to be reconstructed upon a true conception of the life of citizens.

(2) The completion of education must be assumed by the family and the Church. This division and specialization of labor is not out of harmony with a true development and is not impracticable. The incapacity of the State to teach religion does not disqualify it to do good service in its own sphere of secular helpfulness. As Bishop Harris has wisely said: "If the facts were known it would probably be found that in the proper work of the school there is hardly any Christian instruction possible, and that what is given could be better and more efficiently given by the pastor and the parents, in the Church and in the home. It should not be forgotten that Christianity is not a philosophy. It has no peculiar

system of thought or summary of knowledge. It does not profess to teach a peculiar astronomy, or geology, or cosmogony, or ontology, however mistakenly or persistently such a claim has been made for it. Nay, it is now well seen that however valuable dogmas and creeds are and shall be, yet Christianity is not merely a set of dogmas, or creed of opinions, but is a faith, a life. It does its best work, not by dogmatic teaching, not by propounding theories, but by touching the heart, arousing the conscience, awakening the spirit to the unseen realities above it and the immortal dignities before it; by giving to the disciple love to be the moral motive-power of his life, and by training him to walk with his unseen Guide and King. And this it does, not necessarily by invading the schoolroom and inaugurating a special propagandism there, but rather by shedding its radiance over the life of the child, by sanctifying his sabbaths, by the sweet and gentle ministries of the fireside and family circle, by the simple and loving methods of Christian nurture in the Church, the Sunday-school, the home. To be a Christian does not depend upon the amount or kind of philosophy or scientific knowledge we acquire, nor upon the intellectual training and discipline we undergo; but it depends upon the power of our faith, the completeness of our trust, the entireness of our self-surrender to the guidance of Christ and the Holy Spirit. Let the home-training of the child, then, be all that it should be; let his religious discipline be carefully looked after, according to the Church's plan

... and the question of religious teaching in the school will become comparatively unimportant. The real trouble is the neglect of religious education out of the school, rather than within it. It is the godless home and the indifferent, or formal, or unspiritual Church, rather than the secular school, that are dwarfing the religious life of this generation."[24]

3. The spirit of our laws does not prohibit a Christian teacher from imparting the color of his mind and life to those who are his pupils. The prohibition of religious teaching outside of the formal instructions of the school cannot be logically maintained. Consider for a moment what teachers are permitted to do without restriction. They assume to communicate to the child what they believe to be true, without regard to the parent's opinions. They inculcate views on the injurious effects of alcohol which many parents, as manufacturers, venders, and consumers of intoxicants, do not approve; they teach a morality which parents do not embody in their conduct or consider as established science; they proclaim economical principles which fathers do not always accept as true, and sometimes regard as false, pernicious, and destructive of their interests. The State goes farther. It sometimes makes education compulsory. It reaches out its omnipotent arm, takes out of the family a child upon whom a parent's heart is set, places him in a school under social, philosophical, and moral influences which his father may not ap-

[24] The Relation of Christianity to Civil Society (the Bohlen Lectures for 1882), by Bishop Samuel S. Harris, D.D., LL.D., lecture iv.

prove, and sends him home full of new and strange ideas to pronounce judgment upon the sentiments and principles of the parent who has given him his life and supplies his bodily wants. Can the State do all this and exclude religious influence *because* it is religious? Can the State with any show of reason adopt texts filled with the names of Greek and Roman deities, require the pupil to learn them and the attributes assigned to them, and then reject a text because it contains an Anglo-Saxon name for the Deity? Can it require tuition about innumerable gods in whom no one believes, the excuse being that no one does believe in them, and repudiate all instruction about the one God in whom nearly all believe, on the ground that they do believe in Him? I cannot understand how the Bible, read without comment, can be excluded from a public school, or how the voice of a teacher can be silenced when he expresses his personal religious convictions. The State cannot teach religion, but how can it prevent a free man from expressing his convictions? There is more effect of beer than of logic in that Milwaukee dogmatism that fines a teacher for uttering sentiments about God and the soul, but permits him to teach the atomic evolution of the world and that mind is merely a function of the brain.

Christianity is happily not dependent upon the agency of the secular school for its extension. It is probably well for the development of our national life that the schools are beyond ecclesiastical control. The distinctively clerical influence is conservative, rather than progressive, regarding moral wellbeing rather than intellectual advancement. Such, at least, is the testimony of history. And yet it is possible for the secularization of the school to go too far. The State is assuming a wholly new position in excluding religious influences from the schoolroom. Why not let them enjoy the same freedom that other influences do? Political sectarianism would doubtless be as obnoxious to partisans as religious sectarianism can be to any, yet we hear the claim constantly pressed that political science shall be taught in our schools. To exclude on the ground of religion a book or an influence or an exercise from a school seems to me beyond the scope of the State's proper authority. It is persecution of religion *because* it is religion.

The Christian men of this nation will be very weak indeed if they do not insist that the Christian Scriptures and Christian teachers be everywhere accorded the privilege of exposition and utterance. Christian duty binds every disciple of Christ to let the light within him shine upon all around him, most of all upon those whose unshaped lives are submitted to his molding hand. No Christian can desire that our public schools shall be converted into propagandas of a sectarian or dogmatic type. But it may be fairly asked that the influence of Jesus might have its place among the shaping forces; that the young might be taught the fatherhood of God and the brotherhood of men; that veracity, reverence, justice, and charity might be inculcated; that the conceit of the young might be tempered with some respect for the wisdom and goodness of the world's great men, including those mentioned in the Bible; that the arithmetical consciousness which intensifies the selfishness of our age might be touched with some consideration for the rights of others; that the perception of present interests might be accompanied with some realization of permanent and spiritual needs; that rights and duties might be explained in the light of a personal authority that would give them force in a child's mind; that the religious sentiments might find exercise in some simple and elementary but purely voluntary form of worship that would at least preserve the rudimentary instincts with which men are naturally endowed. Religion within such limits may have place in our public schools without violating any principle of our American conception of the State. The rights of the small number of imported atheists, agnostics, and positivists who would oppose such a plan need not be seriously affected. Their offspring might be marked with a designating badge and kept carefully away from all such influence! Upon such a programme Christians of every name might easily unite: and how, in such an atmosphere, would prejudice and sectarianism soften and dissolve, a general fellowship in high objects of faith drawing the coming generations together in the sense of a common brotherhood, leaving free for each the ever-diminishing differences of personal opinion, while preserving "the unity of the spirit in the bond of peace."

VII.

CHRISTIANITY AND THE PROBLEMS OF LEGISLATION.

CHRISTIANITY AND THE PROBLEMS OF LEGISLATION.

I. THE RELATION OF CHRISTIANITY TO THE STATE.
   1. Christianity has no Alliance with Civil Power.
   2. Gladstone's Argument for a State Religion.
   3. The Fruits of State Religions.
   4. Ethical and Doctrinal Failure of State Religions.
   5. The Christian Doctrine of Personality.
   6. The Public Functions of Christian Ministers.

II. LAW AS A SOCIAL FACTOR.
   1. The Nature of a Civil Law.
   2. Law as a Moral Influence.
   3. The Limitation of Legal Influence.
   4. The Origin and Authority of Law.
   5. The Purpose of Law.
   6. The Contrast of Law and Morality.
   7. Theories of the Functions of the State:
      (1) The Theocratic Theory;
      (2) The Paternal Theory;
      (3) The Police Theory;
      (4) The National Theory.

III. THE CHRISTIAN CONCEPTION OF LEGISLATION.
   1. The Element of Personality in Modern Law.
   2. Freedom of Conscience and Freedom of Contract.
   3. The Moral Consciousness as Court of Appeal.
   4. Christianity the Molder of the Moral Consciousness.

VII.

CHRISTIANITY AND THE PROBLEMS OF LEGISLATION.

I.

1. It would be superfluous for me in this presence to recount the history of Christianity in relation to the civil law, or to enumerate the theories that have been held concerning that relation. It is evident that Christianity itself disclaims and repudiates any such relation whatever, except in so far as personal protection is demanded for Christian men in the exercise of their natural and spiritual rights. "My kingdom is not of this world," said Christ, and no crown of temporal sovereignty was ever claimed by him. Paul made no higher demand of the empire which finally adopted the cross as its symbol than mere recognition and protection as a Roman citizen.

2. It is the State rather than the Church that has derived advantage from the historic union of the two. From a philosophic point of view it is not difficult to show some reason for the alliance of legislative with ecclesiastical power. One of the most illustrious of modern statesmen, Mr. Gladstone, says: "Religion is applicable to a state because it is the office of the State, in its personality, to evolve the social life of man, which social life is essentially moral in the ends

it contemplates, in the subject-matter on which it feeds, and in the restraints and motives it requires; and which can only be effectually moral when it is religious." [1] There are two assumptions here which are certainly open to question. The first is the attribution of "personality" to the State, which we have formerly discussed in treating of Dr. Mulford's idea of the nation as a "moral person," and found it to be a fanciful diversion of metaphysics. The second assumption is that the State evolves the social life of man in the moral order, which implies that the individual life is morally ordered by public authority; a proposition which, however it may be regarded in England, must provoke a smile in the United States. But the final objection to Mr. Gladstone's argument for a state religion is the very fact which he adduces in favor of it: that the "social life of man is *essentially moral* in the ends it contemplates, in the subject-matter on which it feeds, and in the restraints and motives it requires." The "restraints" and "motives" offered by the State are not moral, but compulsory. It is precisely because much of the social life of man *is* moral that it cannot be wholly regulated by the State.

3. Before discussing the nature of legislation and the problems with which it deals, let us see how a state religion has affected that "social life of man" which Mr. Gladstone says is "essentially moral." The union of Church and State has led to terrible religious wars, which would never have happened but

[1] Quoted in Woolsey's Political Science, vol. ii.

for the alliance of religion with political power, as the wars with the Albigenses, the Hussite War, the Thirty Years' War, and the English Rebellion. It has forced compliance with offensive ritual and ceremony, destroying personal independence, provoking hypocrisy, and punishing with imprisonment and death sincere recalcitrants. It has shut out from the English parliament men of great ability and patriotism because they were disqualified for taking the communion of the Established Church. For centuries it excluded all dissenters from the privileges of the universities. It has intensified social rancor and directed obliquy against a sincere and spiritually minded class. It has trammeled thought and deadened spirituality by binding the clergy to political favor. It has prevented intermarriage on grounds that were ridiculous. It has caused prosecutions and persecutions innumerable, and made the "spiritual lords" the sport of the serious.

4. Besides these fruits there has been a failure to accomplish the results intended. An established religion has usually neglected the poor, for whose "social life" alone it could be justified, in order to court the rich. It has failed to suppress or even retard the growth of unbelief, and the countries where it exists are precisely those where skepticism has grown most rapidly and is the strongest. Nor has it secured discipline and purity, either doctrinal or practical, even among communicants. Finally, the best attainments of the state churches themselves are prompted by voluntary, rather than legal,

action, as in the sums subscribed for missions. Such are the comments of history upon the doctrine that it is "the office of the State, in its personality, to evolve the social life of man." False in theory, it has proved false in practice, and commends itself to no one so naturally as to a prime minister, in whom the State's "personality" becomes self-conscious.

5. Christianity places responsibility for social progress where alone power to achieve it may be found — in the actual individual persons who constitute the State, not in the State itself, endowed with an imaginary "personality" as powerless in action as it is baseless in thought. What Christianity demands is that each one of those living and responsible persons shall be made to feel that he is one, and that he shall be protected in his inalienable rights of thought and conscience, sheltered under the mighty sword of the civil power, which shall fall upon no man to compel, but only to defend. The mission of Christianity to mankind is not to force, but to win; not to drive, but to draw; not to render masses of men mechanically virtuous, but to render every soul vitally spiritual. The attitude of Christ toward all legislation is shown in his treatment of the Mosaic law. He pointed to himself as its personal fulfilment, and reduced its complex code to one essential principle. Love and personality are Christ's two leading ideas, so far as his life-giving power over men is a matter of ideas at all. Love, crowning and perfecting personality; personality, culminating in love, — these are the fountains of all Christian thought and of all Christian

practice. The perfect love in the perfect person — this is the incarnation toward which creation centred and from which redemption radiates.

But Christianity is not an antinomian influence either in the moral or the political spheres. Personality is the only foundation upon which either moral or civil law can be based. Deny it, and laws of every kind are mere arbitrary rules of expediency. The aim of law is the definition of rights. Rights arise from personality. Only persons can have rights. Love seeks the wellbeing of its object. That wellbeing is attained, with respect to human persons, only when each one has his rights. Love, therefore, is realized only in the light of law. It is for this reason that Christ sums up the law as consisting finally in love, which is the "fulfilling of the law."

6. How, then, is Christianity related to human legislation, to the framing of civil laws? It holds steadily before the eyes of men a truth which they have so often forgotten — the dignity of man. Through its prophets, the ministers of Christ, it ever voices forth this fundamental doctrine, that man, every man, is by nature a moral being, a person with inalienable rights, and bound by correlative duties. Upon this foundation of a community of nature it erects that other truth, that every man should love his neighbor as himself. Lineal successors, not of the priests of the Jewish dispensation, but of the "goodly fellowship" of the glorious Hebrew prophets, the ministers of Christ find it a part of their vocation to denounce wrong, to explain right, to enlighten and

quicken the conscience, and thus to lead the people to the realization of duty. Let them see to it that they magnify their calling, avoiding the perils of partisan entanglement and alliance with political demagogues, pressing fearlessly home upon the people the principles of Christ that underlie our Republican Constitution and have accomplished the fulfilment of that prophecy of our Lord, "The truth shall make you free."

Not, then, by the dictation of statutes, not by forcing its creed or even its morality upon the people, would Christianity extend its influence in the world. To deny or restrict those rights of thought and conscience which it assumes as the cardinal elements of its doctrine would be a suicidal act. Maintaining his own right to representation in the making of laws, and seeing in those laws inherent limitations as affecting personal liberty, a Christian man must not only grant but strive to secure to every other man the equal recognition of his right.

II.

Having outlined the spirit of Christianity toward legislation, let us now briefly consider law as a social factor.

1. "A law," says a distinguished writer on jurisprudence, "is a command proceeding from the supreme political authority of a state and addressed to the persons who are the subjects of that authority."[2] In a state like our American republic, the "supreme

[2] Sheldon Amos's Science of Law, chap. iv.

political authority" is a legislature, state or national, chosen by the suffrages of the adult male population in whom political sovereignty is assumed to reside. We therefore consider ourselves a "self-governed" people, being subjects and sovereigns at once. Nothing would seem at the first glance more easy than the realization of any ideal which the majority might entertain, by the simple process of legislation.

2. That law is a potent social factor in human life, limiting and shaping the activity of all, cannot be denied. A moral constitution of society is, doubtless, anterior to a legal one. It is the source out of which law originates; and yet, as Sheldon Amos says: "Apart from the strength, coherence, and permanence imparted by law and government, the most hopeful moral growths are too frail and feeble to endure, still less to come to maturity."[3] Law reacts upon the people as a pledge to abstinence does upon an inebriate. It creates a standard by which each one judges himself, even though he may not attain to its requirements. "So soon as a law is made and lifted out of the region of controversy, it begins to exercise a moral influence which is no less intense and widespreading for being almost imperceptible. Though law can never attempt to forbid all that is morally wrong, yet that comes to be held to be wrong which the law forbids."[4] When once enacted, the people not only obey a law which they have opposed, but "by a peculiar action of the imagination they will

[3] Amos, op. cit. preface.
[4] Amos, op. cit. chap. xiii.

unconsciously attribute to it a quasi-mysterious origin and banish all memory of the competing views of expediency amidst which it arose." Because of this confessed power of law over life, men are inclined to look to legislation for the panacea of all social ills.

3. But the ameliorating influence of law is not without limitation. There is ample room for the persistence of evil when law has done its utmost to define rights and to cover them with its protection. "A man may be a bad husband, a bad father, a bad guardian, without coming into conflict with the rules of a single law. He may be an extortionate landlord, a wasteful tenant, a hard dealer, an unreliable tradesman, and yet the legal machinery of the country be quite powerless to stimulate or to chastise him. He may be, furthermore, a self-seeking politician, an unscrupulous demagogue, or an indolent aristocrat, and yet satisfy to the utmost the claims of the law upon him. Nevertheless, it is just in the conduct of these several relationships that the bulk of human life consists and on them that national prosperity and honor depend." [5]

4. The reason of the impotency of law to rectify all human ills arising from personal action will appear, if we consider the origin of law and what it is that gives it authority. Civil law has two distinct sources. The first is unconscious custom, which slowly comes to have the force of law in regulating conduct and at last obtains conscious recognition. The second is legislative enactment. It is upon this

---

[5] Amos, op. cit. chap. iii.

that hope rests in the minds of those who expect legislation to reconstruct and perfect human society. But they fail to estimate its precise origin and value. Even in our representative republic, law is not always, as theory would lead us to suppose it must be, the expression of the popular will. It is often dictated by powerful corporations, sometimes by single individuals, usually by the interests of the legislators or a class of their constituents, seldom by a majority of the best qualified electors, and never by the whole people.

Law is always born amid the pains of controversy and is the child of compromise. It almost never embodies the results of pure reason or the highest morality. It affords security for such rights as can probably be enforced and aims at such justice as it is expedient to seek. Considered in its totality, it is simply the expression of the character of the people as a whole, representing what they permit as much as what they desire. Whether originating in custom or enactment, it is seldom better, and is sometimes worse, than the average of the personal wills whose command it purports to be.

The effectiveness of a law is limited by the conditions of its origin. If, by some fortuity, a law is beyond the ability of the average man to observe, it becomes nugatory both in its interpretation and its execution. While the legislator is supposed to regard the wellbeing of the people as a whole, the judge and the executive observe the effect of the law upon the individual in concrete cases. Accordingly, the judge interprets the law and the executive applies it with more regard to the personal conditions of its enforcement. Hence a really bad law either quietly becomes a dead letter, or is soon repealed by a special revolt of the governed.

5. We obtain a new view of the nature of law, if we consider its purpose. It assumes the existence of intelligent and self-determined beings, who possess rights and at the same time are likely to invade one another's rights. Without law there would be the absolute rule of the stronger and the oppression of the weaker. It aims to prevent this collision and to confine each social unit to the sphere of his rights. It would preserve all by restraining each. To this end it defines rights and affixes a penalty to their violation sufficient to prevent their invasion. It first creates a government to serve as the organ of its commands, and defines the sphere and functions of the government in a constitution. It then issues commands for the preservation of the government itself, the freedom of the persons who constitute the State, and the perpetuity of the institutions necessary to the life of the State, such as the family, property, and contract.

With such a purpose, it is evident that law has limits as touching human conduct. It deals only with acts, not with motives; with relations between men, not with the life of individuals. It does not presume to say how fully any man shall realize his own rights, but simply that he shall not invade the rights of others.

6. There is clearly not only a distinction but a perfect contrast between civil law and morality. Law appeals for its enforcement to external compulsion, morality to the conscience and the dignity of moral freedom. Law terrifies and makes men afraid, morality emboldens and makes men brave; law assumes that selfishness is the governing principle of life, morality that justice is more authoritative than self-love; law formulates distinct propositions and precepts whose letter must be obeyed, morality avoids verbal rules and stereotyped maxims, putting love in the place of prohibitions; law regards the overt act, morality the intent of the heart; law estimates rectitude by the non-violation of its prohibitions, morality by the positive character and actions of the man. Clearly, it is not the purpose of law to codify morality, and morality cannot expect universal dominion through the operation of law. If we trace law and morality in their specific applications, we still more distinctly perceive their antithesis. " Law, indeed," says Amos, "marks out the limits of the family and provides general remedies for the grosser violations of its integrity. But it can go, and does go, a very little way toward making good husbands and wives, fathers and mothers, sons and daughters, brothers and sisters. Law can create and define the relations of landlord and tenant, farmer and laborer; but it is well known how little it can do directly to guide landlords in the rent they morally ought to exact, or the compensation for improvements made by an outgoing tenant which they ought to allow, or to compel farmers to remun-

erate their laborers, build cottages for them, and exact work from them in the way least likely to render them paupers in their old age. So with contract. The operations of the market must meet with some other stimulus and guide than legal rules, if men are to be scrupulously honest in keeping engagements, in selling pure and unadulterated goods, in laying bare all the hidden vices of the things for which they are endeavoring to find customers. Law can do none of these things directly. Indeed, by trying to do them directly, it may only weaken that force of morality which alone is equal to the task." [6]

7. Various theories have been held concerning the functions of the State as a moral agency, and these we shall briefly notice.

(1) The theocratic theory assumes that the State is founded upon a moral and religious basis and, therefore, clothes the government with moral and religious authority. This blending of political and religious power has been almost universal in the great historic nations. The priest has usually been the counselor of the ruler, and often the ruler has united the political and spiritual headship of the nation in his own person. Law has fortified itself in the consciences of men by invoking the sanction of morality and religion, aided by the ceremonials of the prevailing faith, returning for this service the protection and compulsion of political power in the enforcement of morals and religious creeds. There are three traits of this conception of the State which unfit it for the modern

[6] Amos, op. cit. chap. iii.

mind: (1) It exalts the political authority to a superhuman height, rendering it absolute and declaring it infallible, while the individual conscience and reason are repressed and silenced. (2) It emasculates the powers of progress by assuming the possession of a final perfection, admitting of no criticism, experiment, or spontaneity. (3) It is harsh and cruel in its judgments, claiming a divine right of retribution in its punishments, exercising an infinite jurisdiction over life with a finite comprehension of its facts and principles. A true theocracy once existed upon the earth, but it soon lapsed into a false one. So long as the Jews retained the theocratic constitution of Moses, they prospered even amidst adversity; but they adopted a monarchy with theocratic pretensions and suffered the consequences of their apostasy.

(2) The paternal theory is a residuum of the monarchical *régime*. A good king is, indeed, in a certain sense "the father of his people." He has their well-being near his heart and ever in his mind. In a kingdom or empire, the analogy of a family is not an unnatural one. But how shall we apply this conception to a republic? Are the "sovereign people" children? Who is the "father of the people"? A father of a family is the agent upon whom the happiness of his children largely depends and he is in a measure responsible for it. A republican State does not hold in its hand the happiness of the people and is not accountable for it. Bluntschli says: "The happiness of men is, for the most part, independent of the State. Even most of the material goods on which

human welfare is dependent, dwellings, food, clothing, and income, are acquired, not through the State, but by the labor and saving of individuals. Still more is this true of the spiritual goods, on which the ideal wealth and happiness of mankind are founded. It is not the State which endows men with their talents and capacities; these are gifts of nature, and they differ in individual cases instead of being common to all. The State can confer on no one the delights of friendship and love, the charm of scientific study, or of poetical and artistic creation, the consolations of religion, or the purity and sanctification of the soul united with God."[7]

(3) The police theory would limit the purpose of the State to the realization of personal liberty in the enjoyment of natural rights. Its sole end is said to be justice. It assumes that each man can best pursue and secure his own happiness, if he is permitted to use without restraint or interference such powers as he may possess for the accomplishment of his own freely chosen ends. Law, as regarded by this theory, is simply a necessary evil, a protection offered to the well-disposed against the rapacity and injustice of the ill-disposed. There is, doubtless, much of truth in this doctrine, but it fails to formulate the whole. While morality and happiness include too much for the State to realize, because both depend largely upon conditions of mind and heart which the State cannot reach or control, justice alone includes too little. This circumscription of the func-

[7] Bluntschli, Allgemeine Staatslehre.

tions of the State wholly overlooks the interests of the people as a whole. Even admitting that the nation is nothing, apart from the individuals who compose it, there are material and intellectual needs which individuals, as such, cannot supply, and not very effectually by voluntary incorporation. Roads, canals, bridges, statistical bureaus, explorations, general defence, and many other things are for the benefit of all, yet would not be privately undertaken by any. The police theory of the State fails to grasp the conception of national life and to realize the existence of public rights and duties. Itself a reaction against the paternalism of the eighteenth century, it has provoked a reaction against its own narrowness that is destined to efface it from the public mind.

(4) The national theory avoids on the one hand the identification of law with morality, which too much extends the sphere of political action; and on the other, the restriction of law to the mere protection of rights, which too much contracts it. There are for every people a possible development and perfection of capacities that can be realized only in a national life. This includes the encouragement of morality and the protection of rights, but involves much more. As the life-task of an individual is to develop his personal powers, so the life-task of a nation is to develop the national resources. This does not include responsibility for the personal welfare of all the members of the State. To care for all is impossible unless the State becomes an omniscient providence, watching over the citizens

with a paternal solicitude. No representative government possesses this attribute, and none can be expected to fill the rôle of father to all the political prodigals. Nor is this necessary to the development of the national life. To establish, maintain, and perfect such institutions and such enterprises as the prosperity of the nation requires — such is the duty of the State. Resolved into its lowest terms, this is simply the care of all the citizens for the welfare of the whole. This is possible, for every citizen may be and ought to be interested in the welfare of the whole nation. To reverse the statement, to say that the State, the abstract and impersonal whole, should be responsible for the happiness of its concrete and personal citizens, is an empty and impossible proposition. We cannot look to the State for our wellbeing; we must ourselves secure the wellbeing of the State. If we say that a part of the sovereign people may look to another part for their welfare; that, for example, the poor may so look to the rich, we forget the co-equal sovereignty on which a representative republic is built, and assign a difference of rights and duties which implies a distinction of social classes. If men are politically equal, a part cannot be the political wards of another part. As soon as a dependent class appears sovereignty vanishes from that class. A "sovereign cannot take tips," cannot ask for *pourboire*, without degradation.[8] The citizens of a representative republic must secure

---

[8] Elaborated by W. G. Sumner, What Social Classes owe to Each Other, chap. ii.

by their strength and wisdom the prosperity of the nation; not gather, like helpless children, about the knees of a parent, asking for bread. In the civil order there is no "father" to meet the "prodigal" on the way; and to kill the "fatted calf" is to rob the industrious brother. When a people imagine such a father in a king, they preface their petition with the scriptural acknowledgment: "Let me be as one of thy hired servants, for I am no more worthy to be called thy son." For a citizen to receive aid from the State, except for actual service rendered, is an abdication of sovereignty.

There are two provinces of human life which legislation alone can never really ameliorate. The first of these is the moral and spiritual life of the soul. The law may, indeed, control outward actions, forcing external compliance with codes and creeds, but it cannot produce that internal consecration to lofty purpose or ennobling faith in which all true morality and religion essentially consist. The other is the production of wealth. Law is not creative. It regulates and conserves, but it does not produce. It may maintain conditions favorable to the creation of wealth, by offering protection to all who put forth productive energies, but it is upon the use of these by the productive agents themselves that all wealth-creation depends. Law may, by its restrictions, cripple and paralyze the industrial energies. It may also redistribute wealth. It may authorize the issue of debased money, it may initiate the creation of public works, it may grant pensions and subsidies to classes of persons, it may even invade the relations of employer and employed and control the division of products; but these actions do not increase wealth, they simply transfer it. The two strong political fanaticisms of our time are the beliefs that the State can make men good, and that the State can make men rich. Both are pernicious, because they are false and because they would carry their falsehood into the field of practice.

III.

1. When we consider that so much of human legislation has been designed to compel men to save their souls by accepting a state religion and to make favored classes rich and powerful at the expense of others, it is not difficult to understand Buckle's opinion that the only progress made in human legislation during the last five hundred years has been made through repealing laws.[9] Freedom of conscience and freedom of contract are the two great legal advances in the history of the world. Both are, in a sense, the triumphs of Christianity, and are simple deductions from its idea of personality. I do not affirm that the idea of personality was unknown to the Roman law, for it was the central idea in that majestic system; but it was a legal abstraction, as much so as the artificial persons, or corporations, which that law recognized. It was Christianity that filled this abstract form with vital ethical contents. Roman law saw a person in a citizen, but none in a

[9] Buckle's History of Civilization, vol. i, chap. v.

slave, a child, or a woman. Christianity at once changed this conception and has reconstructed legislation by its doctrine of the human soul.

2. It seems to me that the interest of Christianity lies in the legal maintenance of these two principles: freedom of conscience and freedom of contract. It will doubtless require brave and vigilant men to defend them, as it has to win them, for humanity.

But there are limits to personal freedom, because the freedom of one may invade the freedom of another. Are men to speak and act without restraint? That would be anarchy. If men were to propose and advocate the erection of temples to Aphrodite and to revive her impure worship, on the pretext of religious faith and ceremonial, would it be disregarding the freedom of conscience to prohibit them? If others were to employ children to labor for a pittance at unhealthy toil and for unnatural hours, would it be a violation of the freedom of contract to forbid them? The real problem of legislation is to find the circumference of personal rights that surrounds each person and to draw the line of prohibition there.

When we make laws to suppress the publication of obscene books and pictures, it is because the young and susceptible have rights as well as writers and publishers. When we desire rigid divorce legislation, it is because helpless women and innocent children have rights as well as sensual men. When the legal regulation of the manufacture and sale of intoxicants is proposed, it is because wives and children and fathers and mothers and taxpayers have rights as well as brewers and distillers and dealers.

3. It is not my purpose to attempt the solution of these practical problems of legislation, so delicate and difficult as to tax the powers of the most expert statesmen; to judge between "overlegislation" and "*laissez faire* run mad;" to discuss the respective merits of "prohibition" and "high license;" or to finish in a paragraph the work of a generation. These are problems that will ultimately find their solution in the moral consciousness of a great people, coming again and again to their discussion with ever-enlarging experience and ever-increased wisdom. The important consideration is that *it is in the moral consciousness of the people that the solution will be found at last.*

An ancient Chinese legend runs: "The three great religious teachers of the Celestial Empire, from their heavenly abode beholding with profound sorrow the degeneracy of their people, and mourning that their lifework seemed so entire a failure, returned to the earth in order to find some suitable missionary whom they could send forth as a reformer. They came in their wanderings to an old man sitting as a guardian of a fountain. He talked to them so wisely and so earnestly of the great concerns which they had most at heart, that they came to the conclusion that he was the very man for the work which they wished to accomplish. But when they proposed the mission to him, he replied: 'It is the upper part of me only that is of flesh and blood; the lower part is of stone. I can talk about virtue and good works, but I cannot rise from my seat to perform any righteous acts.'"

The apologue well pictures human legislation, which can discuss virtue but cannot enforce it. Powerless to realize its own ideals, it needs the animation of a superior life to impart activity. It requires the cure of its moral petrifaction and awaits the words of the divine Master: "Rise and follow me."

4. The most powerful tonic influence felt by the moral consciousness of mankind to-day is the religion of Christ. Wherever its hopes and conceptions penetrate, a moral change speedily follows. Wherever they are temporarily or partially repudiated, there is retrogression. While Christianity does not demand incorporation in the State as an established religion, and does not claim to dictate the specific laws that shall govern men, it does create the spirit out of which better laws proceed. We are slowly shaping on this continent a people who love law, because it is their will to obey it, and who, with power to destroy it, are united to preserve it. For a Christian people, lawmaking is the definition of rights whose reality and sacredness are based upon the exalted conception of a person who is at once the brother of Christ and the son of God. Let this conception suffer a collapse into a materialistic or dynamic one, devoid of spiritual content, and we shall find legislation reduced to a mere conflict of interests and dominated at last by mere brute power. Our representative republic of self-governed persons is the wonder of the world and the paradox of prophecy. Its vital secret is the Christian conception of man that is assumed in its Constitution and legislation. If ever that should

change and cease to be the controlling idea of our national life, we should realize what it is so easy even for statesmen to forget, that the power of our Constitution is a moral power. The chief source of that power is in the religion of Jesus Christ, the ideals of which are creating a nation whose outer form shall be a republic of free men and whose inner life shall be the presence in the soul of God's coming kingdom.

VIII.

CHRISTIANITY AND THE PROBLEMS OF REPRESSION.

CHRISTIANITY AND THE PROBLEMS OF REPRESSION.

I. THE RIGHT OF SOCIETY TO PUNISH.
1. Two Theories of Punishment.
2. Punishment is not ethically based on Retribution.
3. Punishment is not ethically based on Utility.
4. Punishment is ethically based on Repression.
5. Effects of the Christian Conception of Punishment.

II. THE NATURAL HISTORY OF CRIME.
1. What is Crime?
2. The Law of Heredity.
3. Idleness and Poverty.
4. Ignorance, Literary and Industrial.
5. Intemperance.
6. Hopelessness.
7. The Prevention and Cure of Crime.

III. SUMMARY AND CONCLUSION.
1. Summary.
2. Conclusion.

VIII.

CHRISTIANITY AND THE PROBLEMS OF REPRESSION.

I.

A LAW is not simply a definition of rights; it carries consequences to the law-breaker. Fine, imprisonment, and death are the penalties attached to the violation of laws. Without such penalties laws would be as inoperative as a popular vote that all men should be virtuous. What right has a society of equals, through its government, to take from a man his money, his liberty, or his life, because he has not obeyed its commands?

1. Two opposite opinions have been held by high authorities in morals and jurisprudence. Says Immanuel Kant: "If civil society should dissolve itself with the consent of all its members, the last murderer who should be found in prison ought first to be executed, in order that each might bear the penalty of his conduct and that the blood shed by him might not fall upon a people who had not inflicted that punishment."[1] This implies that society possesses a retributive function. Romagnosi, on the contrary, says: "If the right of punishment belongs to soci-

[1] Kant, Metaphysische Anfangsgründe der Rechtslehre.

ety, it is only because of its effects upon the future." [2] Punishment is here regarded as wholly preventive. The doctrine of retribution looks only to the past, that of prevention only to the future. Between them is a vast moral distance and the present is left wholly out of view. The one bases penalty upon the moral law and conceives society to be its executive. The other views punishment as required by social utility, without claiming a moral authority. Must we choose between this transcendentalism of Kant and this utilitarianism of Bentham?

2. I have already, in speaking of the relation between religion and government, expressed dissent from the doctrine which regards the State as the agent of religion and morality. Protection to religion and morality the State should grant; observance of them is beyond its power of enforcement. It cannot make men morally good. Even the infliction of penalty does not assume this. A murderer is no better for hanging. But does retributive power belong to civil law? The moral law is for the conscience, its rebuke is addressed to the motive, its expiation is in remorse, its deliverance is in repentance. Note the contrast with human enactments. The penal law is for the protection of rights, its rebuke is addressed to the overt act, its expiation is in a series of sensations; there is no deliverance until the sentence is fulfilled. In the view of moral law, confession is a step toward

---

[2] Romagnosi, Genese du Droit Penal, vol. i, chapitre xi. This is also the doctrine of Bentham, Introduction to the Principles of Morals and Legislation, chap. xiii; and of Beccaria, Traite des Delits et des Peines, ii.

pardon; in the view of penal law, confession dooms to punishment. Of moral guilt, no other person than the offender can be the judge; of penal guilt another must judge. Because moral law and penal law are in most points different, and in some antithetical, penal judgment cannot be moral retribution. "Vengeance is mine; I will repay, saith the Lord," is a declaration that human punishment, whether individual or social, cannot claim a retributive element. The Creator has not delegated to man the difficult, the delicate, the impossible task of measuring and awarding moral retribution. If he had, the penalty once paid, the sin would be expiated, and every released prisoner would be an innocent man.

3. Will the theory that the right to punish arises from social utility bear examination? It may be "useful" to society that all criminals of every grade, and paupers also, be carried out to sea and thrown overboard into its depths. The problems of crime and pauperism would thus cease to vex the public mind. Wherein does this solution fail? It overlooks the fact that even criminals are persons, endowed with the rights of personality. Does social utility, then, meet with no limitation? May society, to serve its own social needs, justly deprive men of property and liberty and life? There is somewhere a limit to the authority of social utility. Utility has the same defect in justifying penalty that it has as a standard of moral conduct. It is incalculable, incapable of being a criterion. In the sphere of punishment, utility has a further difficulty. The government

practically identifies its own interest with the interest of society. In the name of "utility," the egoism of the State crushes out the freedom of the individual. A critic, an opponent, a recalcitrant, is naturally contemplated as an enemy, whose existence is prejudicial to the interest of the State. A democracy offers but little relief from this tendency to official outrage. The tyranny of a multitude is even more fierce and pitiless than the tyranny of one man. The interest of society, as conceived by itself, at one time prepares the guillotine for a Louis, at another, and sometimes soon, it prepares the same instrument for a Robespierre. If no good man had ever been a martyr to public utility, the emptiness of it as a justification of punishment might be less apparent; but from Socrates to Christ, from Christ to Savonarola, from Savonarola to the latest victim of mob violence, the long line of martyrs rise to refute the maxim, "The voice of the people is the voice of God." Not for his own interest, not for society's interest, not for mere interest of any kind, may another justly take away my life.

4. What, then, justifies the infliction of punishment? Retribution assumes too much, utility, too little. The union of the two will possess no increment of gain. And yet there is a basis, and it must be a moral basis, for this highest of social functions. So long as one of its members uses his powers for their natural ends, without interference with others, society cannot punish him for his sins or bend him to its fancied utilities. The frontier of my personality

must be safe from invasion, or my right to cross the boundaries of another's right cannot be questioned. But the duty of society to protect rights carries with it the authority to repress the invasion of rights. The right of restraint, the right of commanding the peace, this is the moral basis of the right of society to punish. As Jourdan says: "So far as it supposes a superior judge and an infallible justice, the right of punishment does not exist; human justice is not a delegation of divine justice; it overleaps itself when it attempts to punish, it simply represses. The right to punish is simply the legitimate faculty of exercising upon that one who has violated right a restraint whose object is to impose on him respect for right by force; it has its only and true foundation in the superior notion of right, without which society is only a material fact, destitute of all morality."[3] The supposition that God has delegated a retributive power to man is a tradition that has descended from that theocratic age when God was believed to govern through men directly, because he inspired their judgments and their acts. The idea that social utility justifies punishment is a subterfuge of that unethical and materialistic philosophy that has taxed its ingenuity to justify the necessary processes of a moral order while theoretically denying the existence of moral beings. That human punishment is simply forcible restraint from wrong-doing is a moral conception that follows by logical necessity from the Christian idea of men as moral persons. The hand

---

[3] Jourdan, La Justice Criminelle en France, titre i, chapitre i.

that inflicts injury must repair the injury; the life that destroys other life must surrender itself. If punishment were expiation, the hand that robbed would be a guiltless hand when it had restored; the life that had slain its fellow-life would be stainless when the fatal drop had fallen from the scaffold. But the robber and the murderer have still their unsettled accounts with God. To be restrained from crime by a penalty that will henceforth destroy its motive in one's self, a criminal himself might feel is just; but it would fill one with the emotions of a martyr to hear the judge say, in the words once used to an English horse-thief: "You are sentenced to be hanged, not because you stole the horse, but in order to prevent others from stealing horses"!

5. It is the Christian conception of punishment, growing out of the Christian conception of personality, that has transformed the penal statutes of the civilized world and modified the whole treatment of criminals. Our Anglo-Saxon ancestors administered an heroic justice. Besides death, fines, and flogging, mutilation was a common punishment; men were branded on the forehead; their hands, feet, and tongues were cut off; and after the Danish invasion still more horrible mutilations were practised. For the greater offences eyes were plucked out; the nose, ears, and lips were cut off; the scalp was torn away; a female slave guilty of theft was burned alive; and men were even flayed alive. One of Ethelred's stern statutes read: "Let the culprit be smitten till his neck break." Besides these horrors, too painful for

extended recital, the prison outrages against which John Howard directed his crusade were tender mercies. But now the whole picture of judicial barbarity, with the debtor's prison, the whipping-post, and the other paraphernalia of savagery has ceased to haunt us as reality, and is but a gloomy chapter in the history of moral evolution. The pendulum has swung to the other side of its arc, and now that we have "those excellent model prisons which leave little to be desired in construction and in the comfort of the inmates, and many of which under humane management soften the rigors of imprisonment by means of libraries, entertaining lectures and readings, concerts, holidays, anniversary dinners, flowers, and marks for obedience to rules, which shorten the term of confinement," it is seriously asked: "Do these reformed prisons reform?" They certainly do not annihilate crime, but they treat men and women like human beings, and thus in many cases doubtless give the first impressions that they are such which these unfortunates have ever received. If society can teach a portion of its culprits that the humanity they are required to respect is in them also, if it can create in them the Christian conception of personality by disclosing it within themselves, a great and fruitful advance has, no doubt, been made. If you take the criminal young enough, before he has become hardened, before impulse has settled into habit and habit has condensed into character, he is capable of reformation. The thirty-four reformatories in the United States have received nearly one hundred thousand boys and girls, and of these, three fourths, or about seventy thousand, are reported as reformed, at a cost of $150 each per annum.

II.

If crime is not an indestructible necessity, the question of its repression points to the study of its natural history.

1. What is crime? Morality and legislation give different answers. For morality, what is a crime to-day is a crime forever. For legislation, the crime of yesterday may be the virtue of to-morrow. The law of God is unchangeable. The law of the State is variable. The reformer may be regarded as a criminal by the State, but the heresy or treason which is punished as a crime to-day becomes the rallying-cry or the constitutional right of the next generation. On the other hand, the virtues of primitive man are the legal crimes of to-day. The craft and cruelty, the murder and plunder that made him a hero and a chief are now punishable crimes upon the statute-books of every civilized land. In the eye of the law that is a crime which the law prohibits, and nothing else is. But law aims to prohibit that which, in the estimation of each age, is an infringement of recognized rights.

The first cause of crime is evidently an untrained animal instinct, the survival of a tendency to disregard rights and behave as if they were not. Whence comes this? In one sense crime is simply action out of harmony with the environments, last century's practice running wild in this, an ancestral habit that persists in spite of social advancement. Pike, in his "History of Crime," gives this example: "Cruelty is one of the most strongly marked characteristics of the savage. To inflict torture is one of his greatest delights. As soon as he makes a little progress his previous tendencies show themselves in the horrible ferocity of his punishments for criminals. In the course of ages man becomes gradually more merciful. He ceases to mutilate, and even to torture, his fellows. He puts off his savage nature more and more, and learns to pride himself on his civilization; he perceives that even the inferior animals may suffer; and, as suffering has become associated with compassion, he extends his sympathy to all that feel."[4] At last we reach a point where even brutes are protected, some sympathetic Bergh leading legislation to the rescue of unhappy horses and canine waifs. "Naturalists of the modern school point out primitive organisms which still survive in their original form, though new species may have developed out of them. In the same manner there are savages still living among us of the same blood and origin as ourselves and yet unlike us in all except in our common ancestry."[5] The idea that each individual lives over in rude outline the history of his race also finds application here. "The young human being, in the process of attaining the full maturity of his animal powers, has a strong tendency to exhibit in action

[4] Pike's History of Crime in England, vol. ii, chap. xiii.
[5] Pike, op. cit.

the lawless and cruel instincts of his savage ancestors. A healthy boy has a pugnacity and a love of destruction which not uncommonly assume the form of cruelty. It is difficult to teach him honesty with respect to many things he covets. Just like the savage who has advanced one stage, he makes a slave of a younger or weaker boy. In him the partisanship of family, tribe, guild, or clan is intensely strong and, as he reaches adolescence, shows itself in such rough shapes as the apprentice riots of old in London, or the town and gown combats and 'rushes' of modern times at the universities."[6]

2. Thus the jurist as well as the theologian must take account of the great law of heredity that links us with the ancestral past and forces through our veins the dark current of sin that is not original with us, but flows from that primal fount which is sin's first original. And yet we must not empty the whole cup of guilt upon this stream of heredity. In his visit to that "cradle of crime," the home of the criminal clan, the "Jukes," in New York State, Robert Dugdale discovered a nest of thieves, felons, and prostitutes, the picture of which produces a shudder in the mind of one who recalls it.[7] He has traced the growth of that family in a genealogical tree, whose roots reach back to the shameless Margaret, the "mother of crime," — truly a tree of the knowledge of good and evil, whose fruits have been disease and death, — and yet upon that sin-blasted and withered

---

[6] Pike, op. cit.

[7] See The Jukes, by R. L. Dugdale.

tree there are branches of "honesty," "industry," and "temperance" that are even more startling, when we consider their origin, than those scions of shame with which they are intertwined in the close embrace of brotherhood. The percentage of criminals in that fated family is appalling, but here and there a respectable man rises as a protest against that fanaticism of fatality that would always look behind the sinner for his sin. When a "Juke" can become respectable it seems insolent in us to speak reproachfully of that unfortunate Adam, or these ancestral savages, whose posterity have too often striven to conceal their guilt under the credentials of their lineage. A note of necessity seems, however, to lie in this, that nearly all the crime that is committed is done by persons from twenty-five to forty-five years old, marking this period of twenty years, as what jurists call "the criminal age." But the volitional element in crime becomes evident the moment we consider that this maturity marks a voluntary progress requiring years to develop into a life of crime, and that between the cradle and adolescence lies that golden age of innocence, when children, though born of criminal parents and with all their hereditary savagery strong within them, have not yet become the devotees of crime. From thirty-five on to the end of life the proportion of crime gradually diminishes, and but seven per cent. is committed by persons over sixty-five years of age. Is it because it is found that "the way of the transgressor is hard," or is it that "the wages of sin is death"?

3. "The tendency to commit the great majority

of the acts which are now commonly described as crimes, and especially crimes of violence, is at its greatest strength just before, and at the time when, the human being attains the full development of his physical powers."[8] What is it that transforms the golden age of innocence, the period in which the child is incapable of crime, into that career of criminality that reaches its climax just when volition and intelligence are the best developed? I know of no deeper psychological truth than that expressed in the old proverb: "An idle brain is the devil's workshop." Statistics show that eighty per cent. of the convicted criminals never learned a trade. It is estimated that ninety-five per cent. of the street-begging is done by and for those who could earn their living if they were industrious. The first school of crime is mendicancy. Little children are pressed into it, and from beggars lapse into thieves. The crimes against property are nearly ninety per cent. of the whole number, which reveals the relation between crime and pauperism. The spontaneous activity of a child is capable of direction, but will find its field in crime if not addressed to industry. The occupied have little time to plan and execute wrong, and the fruits of honest labor remove the temptation to commit it. Idleness and poverty are inseparably connected, and the criminal class is constantly recruited from the pauper class at every stage of its development. The possession of property transforms the owner, develops his

[8] Pike, op. cit.

sense of justice, creates in him respect for rights by reminding him that he himself has them, and renders him responsible for his conduct. I heard Fred Douglass say that, in his opinion, the only hope of the enfranchised American negroes lies in their becoming property owners. A careful inspection of prisons shows that the most of their inmates have never owned property. It was a Jewish proverb that "Whosoever does not teach his son a trade is as if he brought him up to be a robber." With all their defections, the sons of Israel have seldom been criminals. The mere tradition of industry has barred the path to the prison.

4. I am doubtful whether poverty is the greater cause of ignorance or ignorance the greater cause of poverty. Like disease and death, they seem to produce each other by a reciprocal infection. Of the ten thousand inmates of the almshouses in New York, thirty-two per cent. could neither read nor write; only twenty-four per cent. could both read and write. But the connection of ignorance and crime is not so close as that of ignorance and poverty. It is mainly through poverty that ignorance affects the increase of criminals. Only about twenty per cent. of the prisoners in the Eastern Penitentiary in Pennsylvania had never attended school. The worst grades of criminals show about this average. But the percentage of criminals who have never learned a trade is four times as high as the percentage of those who have never been to school. Nearly one half of the prisoners just referred to

were children of mechanics, honest men, who had failed to give their offspring a means of earning a livelihood. It is not literary ignorance that makes criminals. The education of the schools, if it does not shape those who receive it in right ways, renders them more efficient and skilful in crime, more able to avoid detection or to effect escape from justice, but constitutes no preventive check on the augmentation of the criminal class. It is the moral and religious element in school-training that curbs the criminal tendencies and so prevents the birth of crime in the learner. It is this element that a large number of our modern theorists are striving vigorously to drive from our public schools.

5. The darkest lines in this sombre picture of the natural history of crime are those in which we trace the effects of intemperance. No one can touch this topic without being exposed to one of two dangers: one of shrinking from a theme so travestied because it is so hackneyed; the other of joining in the intemperate zeal which would banish even from the holy communion the wine that symbolizes the warming life of atoning blood, which refers all sin to intoxicants, and makes their use the one scapegoat vice whose banishment is to bear all human guilt into the wilderness of oblivion. I do not understand how a distinguished English baronet could write a learned book on the "The Punishment and Prevention of Crime"[a] and never once refer to intemperance as a cause, or temperance reform as

---

[a] The Punishment and Prevention of Crime, by Sir Edmund F. Du Cane.

a cure, of the disease whose pathology he describes. Nor do I see how a sane man can imagine that, if all intoxicants were swept from the earth to-day, there would be no crime in the world to-morrow. More than two centuries ago, a calm jurist of vast experience, Sir Matthew Hale, said: "If the murders and manslaughters, the burglaries and robberies, the riots and tumults . . . and other enormities that have happened in my time were divided into five classes, four of them would be seen to have been the issue and product of excessive drinking, of tavern and alehouse drinking." [10] Carefully collated statistics show that from eighty to ninety per cent. of the crimes committed still have some connection with intemperate drinking. The indictment against intoxicants is strong enough, without incurring the charge of fanaticism and the humiliation of refutation, to justify the sober assertion that the traffic that makes drunkards is responsible for four fifths of the crime committed in civilized lands, and should be made to bear its burdens. Should be made to bear its burdens, did I say? Nay, should be prohibited from its work of wreck and ruin. That the right of society to repress crime justifies the repression of crime's most prolific cause is too axiomatic to require discussion.

6. But there is working in the nature of man a deeper and more subtle power of destruction than lies concealed in the drunkard's cup. It is the cause of which recourse to inebriation is but one of the

[10] Quoted by A. J. F. Behrends, Socialism and Christianity, chap. ix.

effects. Why does a man seek the stupor or the exhilaration of intoxication? Is it not usually a desolation of spirit, a hopelessness of heart, that finds the customary level of life dreary, and the future as empty as the present? Some study of the psychology of inebriety has convinced me that, apart from physical disease, despair of life, temporary or permanent, is the secret cause of drunkenness. It is the condition of those "who are strangers from the covenants of promise, having no hope, and without God in the world." If pessimism is possible as a philosophy, how common and how potent it must be as an impulse! It is a perilous state when one considers life as chaff and emptiness. Disappointment, bereavement, and loss often induce this feeling. He who acts in such a mood, unrestrained by the bonds of a holy faith, or a fixed habit of caution, or a governing principle of rectitude, is in danger of falling into crime. Its deepest cause is moral recklessness, resulting from an unsatisfied spirit.

7. If we seek the means of preventing and curing crime, we think at once of industrial occupation, education, and temperance — the world's remedies. They are only antidotes for symptoms, not cures of the disease, or even sure preventives of it. What is to make men industrious, intelligent, and temperate? To what end is industry, if all terminates in dust and ashes? To what purpose is intelligence, if it simply increases our knowledge of the evil in the world? Why should a man be sober, if his powers are all to

crumble to decay to-morrow? A flippant optimism may laugh at these questions and ridicule them as foolish, but a flippant optimist is likely to be too superficial to assume the rôle of ridicule with impunity. If certain current ideas, philosophic and popular, of the nature and destiny of man are true, these are not only serious but forcible questions. On that supposition, I doubt if they can be answered with any stronger argument than ridicule. Whence comes the motive to be industrious, intelligent, and temperate? There is a philosophy of life that would make all men criminals at heart, only waiting for the opportunity of action, if it were universally accepted. The true source of the motives that make men industrious, intelligent in any desirable sense, and temperate in their habits, is the conception and estimate of man presented by Christianity. I do not say that there are no men who possess virtues, who have not built them on this conception, because I recognize the fact that much of what passes for human virtue is compliance with social custom, the fruit of long-continued habit and of imitation. Much of our life is instinctive and automatic. There is a heredity of good, as well as a heredity of evil. What I mean to assert is that when the impulse to crime arises, its restraint, apart from mere fear, is found in some motive that springs out of the conception of man which is most distinctly taught by Jesus Christ. Others have, in part, held that conception, even before his day, and many since, without connecting it with a thought of him; but it is, nevertheless, his idea of man. The natural history of crime is simply this: "Every man is tempted, when he is drawn away of his own lust and enticed. Then, when lust hath conceived, it bringeth forth sin; and sin, when it is finished, bringeth forth death." The only power that can arrest that process, when it is begun, is the picture, in the soul, of man as Christ has portrayed him. Sometimes that sense of what we are, and what Christ's ideal is, flashes upon the mind as the blinding light that smote Saul to the earth when he rode to Damascus, sometimes it dawns as gently as the breaking of morning light upon the hilltops. Until it comes, the possibility of crime is an open pathway that needs only the sufficient enticement at its end to lure the footsteps into it. This is no mysticism that I am uttering. It is the plain truth that, without a right conception of man and his relations to God, it is merely an accident if one is not a criminal. But many men have this and yet some of them are led to crime. There is needed one other security, the disposition to realize this high conception. The diathesis of moral disease must be superseded by the thrill of spiritual life. This is God's gift. "Ye will not come unto me, that ye might have life," said Christ. Christianity teaches that the final preventive and cure of human sin is in the regeneration of men through Christ as a Saviour. The world is striving to solve the problem of human sinfulness, which is the fountain of human crime, by work and knowledge and temperance. It will fail. Its psychology is superficial. Like a physician who represses symptoms and allows the disease to result in death, it works upon the surface and leaves untouched the secret cause of crime. The mission of the Church is to apply the method of the world's Saviour and to cleanse the stream by the purification of the fountain. Evangelical work goes deeper than all humanitarian reforms and looks for the reformation of the outward life through the renovation of the heart.

III.

1. We have now examined the relation of Christianity to the leading problems of society. We have found everywhere Christ's conception of man throwing light upon these problems. If the laborer has rights, it is because he is endowed with personality. If the distribution of wealth is possible upon other grounds than the rule of the strongest, it is because these personal rights radiate outward from the man and project themselves in the sphere of property. If marriage and the family are to be preserved to society, it is through the recognition of personal rights in the domestic circle. If education is to receive its perfection in the complete unfolding of human powers, the spiritual and moral nature of man must be regarded. If legislation is to embody justice and realize liberty, it must postulate the doctrine of personal freedom and of rights and duties as the ground of freedom. Finally, if crime is to be repressed and extirpated, the moral regeneration of men must be accepted as possible and the universal reign of mechanical necessity must be denied.

2. The relation of Christianity to these problems is

briefly this: it carries the master-key that unlocks every one of them; that master-key is Christ's conception of man. I bring the question to this issue: let what Christ has taught of man's nature and destiny be denied; let the mind picture society as an organism whose constituents are impersonal automata, mechanical products of matter and its forces, infinitely complex, but still governed by the law of physical fatality; let the fact of personality be rejected and the reality of inherent rights be contradicted; and I affirm that, when men universally believe this, social order will have no existence, the physically weaker will go down in the struggle for life under the remorseless competition of the stronger, and the human race will be plunged into a general pandemonium. Every disruption of social order that has lately startled the fears of men has originated from some phase of this chain of assumptions. On the other hand, let all that Christ has taught be admitted; let it be assumed that each personal being is endowed with inherent rights and immortal life; let it be conceded that the human brotherhood is linked together under the laws of a moral order and the providence of a beneficent Father; — and an ideal state will be realized among men. In the light of that contrast, I venture the assertion that, if ever an ideal order is realized by humanity, it will be under the leadership of the Christian conception of man and will require that for its basis. The current agitation of mind over social questions is the best token that the hearts and consciences of men are stirred as they never have been stirred before; and it requires little insight to discover that the postulates underlying the discussion of social problems and the hopes of social amelioration are derived from the teachings of Christ, however illogical and grotesque some of their applications may seem to be. Christus Redemptor has, with atoning sacrifice, brought forgiveness of sin to the great company of the redeemed. Christus Consolator has stanched the tears of the world's sorrow and filled the hearts of the afflicted and the wronged with immortal hope. Christus Consummator will establish the kingdom of God in the hearts of men and transform human society at last into an order of final perfection. And you of this noble School of the Prophets, soon to go forth as heralds of that coming kingdom, have a work more vital to the progress of social regeneration than that of any economist or jurist or social reformer of your time. Your part may seem humble and your reward not very great, but it will not be so in the final estimate of eternal values, "for all things are yours, . . . whether the world, or life, or death, or things present, or things to come; all are yours; and ye are Christ's; and Christ is God's."

THE END.

www.ingramcontent.com/pod-product-compliance
Lightning Source LLC
Chambersburg PA
CBHW021816230426
43669CB00008B/766